"For women now old and for all women growing imperceptibly and/or perceptibly older—and that includes all of us—take up this book for an enjoyable, enlightening reading experience. Not a densely scholarly collection, it is rather a marvelous gathering together across a broadly interdisciplinary range of . . . insightful . . . pieces exploring an area that women's scholarship has generally . . . ignored. There is much to learn, to surprise, and to excite our concern in these pages."
Jacqueline D. Goodchilds, PhD, Professor, Department of Psychology, University of California at Los Angeles

"Offers a fresh, insightful, and eye-opening feminist look at the realities of old age and ageism. A jargon-free, readable collection, it sounds an important call for liberatory attitudinal change."
Josephine Donovan, PhD, Professor, English Department, University of Maine, Orono, Maine;
Author of Feminist Theory

"A laudable opening up of dialogue between younger and older women, particularly useful in women's studies introductory or issue-focused courses. Aging women's voices and concerns are projectd with the belief and knowledge that growth and change continue in the last stages of life and that open discussion promotes self-possession and decision-making, as well as political analysis. The [chapters] should speak to older women who share the experiences of the authors."
Nancy Porter, PhD (cand.), Associate Professor, Department of English, Portland State University, Portland, Oregon

Women, Aging and Ageism

Women, Aging and Ageism

Evelyn R. Rosenthal
Editor

Women, Aging and Ageism was simultaneously issued by The Haworth Press, Inc., under the same title, as a special issue of the *Journal of Women & Aging*, Volume 2, Number 2 1990.

Harrington Park Press
New York • London

ISBN 0-918373-73-6

Published by

Harrington Park Press, 10 Alice Street, Binghamton, NY 13904-1580
EUROSPAN/Harrington, 3 Henrietta Street, London WC2E 8LU England

Harrington Park Press is a subsidiary of The Haworth Press, Inc., 10 Alice Street, Binghamton, NY 13904-1580.

Women, Aging and Ageism was originally published as *Journal of Women & Aging*, Volume 2, Number 2 1990.

Cover design by Marshall Andrews.

Library of Congress Cataloging-in-Publication Data

Women, aging, and ageism / Evelyn R. Rosenthal, editor.
    p. cm.
    "Originally published as Journal of women & aging, volume 2, number 2, 1990" — T.p. verso.
    Includes bibliographical references.
    ISBN 0-918393-73-6 (pbk. : acid-free paper)
    1. Aged women—United States. 2. Aging—United States. 3. Ageism—United States. I. Rosenthal, Evelyn R.
HQ1064.U5W597 1990
305.4'0973—dc20

90-4643
CIP

CONTENTS

ALL HAWORTH BOOKS & JOURNALS
ARE PRINTED ON CERTIFIED
ACID-FREE PAPER

ABOUT THE EDITOR

Evelyn R. Rosenthal, PhD, is Associate Professor and Director of the Division of Career and Interdisciplinary Studies in the School of Education and Human Development at the State University of New York at Binghamton. She has written widely on working women of all ages, and her current research documents the lives of retired women workers across social classes and ethnic groups. Dr. Rosenthal founded the Women's Studies Program at SUNY-Binghamton and is a co-founder of both the National Women's Studies Association and the New York State Women's Studies Association. She earned her doctorate in sociology from Cornell University.

Preface

This is not your typical academic volume on aging women. You will look in vain for esoteric measures of arcane variables and other paraphernalia of scholarly discourse. But neither is it a popular pot boiler on how to grow old gracefully. This is a book written by professionals who are deeply concerned about women and aging and who want to share their hard-earned insights with others who teach about or provide services to older women, or who simply want to know more about the experience of growing old in America today.

To read this collection is to engage on a voyage of self-discovery even as we enter the worlds of other women. For what you will find here are essays written with passion, going to the heart of the female experience, and finding there some crucial lesson for us all. There is no pretense to some value-free objective position from which to analyse the material drawn from "real life." To the contrary, the chapters are informed by a feminist consciousness, an awareness that gender makes a difference in how a person is perceived and in what choices are possible. But just as feminist scholarship in general has moved from a simplistic focus on sex differences to a more nuanced view of gender as an essential element of social structure rather than a characteristic of individuals, so, too, the essays in this collection deal with the intersection of women's lives and the gendered social structures of our society.

There is a second dimension along which this volume represents a novel departure; namely, the integration of disciplinary perspectives. The authors represent a variety of fields of study and action—academe and practice, social sciences and the humanities, education and the arts. This inclusiveness is another hallmark of the new feminist scholarship, and the underlying rationale for that academic hybrid, Women's Studies. But this should be a model for the study of the life course in general; men, no less than women, lead multifaceted existences. It is only the academy that insists on truncating the human experience.

Here, also, is where the study of aging and of gender follow a similar course: both of necessity are cross-disciplinary. Biology, psychology, sociology, political science, economics, and the humanities all contribute crucial insights to an understanding of the experience of growing old and of being gendered. Aging is a process, yes, but one that resembles a mosaic rather than a continuum. And something of this multifaceted reality is reflected in this collection.

I should add, finally, that I have a special interest in books such as this one — which in itself turns out to be a lesson in aging. As a relatively old graduate student in the 1960s, I had the great good luck to work with Matilda White Riley on the three pathbreaking volumes of *Aging and Society* (Russell Sage Foundation, 1968, 1969, 1972). During the five years of this project, I also was greatly influenced by the New Feminist Movement, so that by the early 1970s when I had achieved some visibility in the field of social gerontology, I became aware, along with many others (and especially Carroll Estes and Vivian Woods) that researchers and theorists had managed to ignore one cardinal reality of growing old: that more women than men survived to old age in modern industrial societies, and that the existing literature failed to reflect this fact. Our proudest moment came in the early 1970s, when we organized a potential boycott of a planned annual meeting of the Gerontological Society in a state that had not ratified the Equal Rights Amendment. This was the first public flexing of a feminist muscle in the sacred precincts of what had considered itself a "scientific" (read, objective, impartial, etc.) association. Our actions shocked the reigning powers, but enough members had signed our petitions that the meetings were moved to another state.

Although a change of venue was the immediate goal, our long term agenda was the incorporation of gender into all future studies of aging. At this moment, I think we can say that it is a rare gerontologist indeed who fails to take gender into account in doing research, although in their zeal to appear nonsexist, many will speak of "the older person," sex unspecified. Nonetheless, social gerontology today is something very different from what passed under that heading less than two decades ago.

It is with a sense of maternal pride, then, that I welcome this most recent addition to our understanding of growing old female.

Beth B. Hess, PhD

Women and Varieties of Ageism

Evelyn R. Rosenthal, PhD

Powerful myths and stereotypes of aging limit the lives of middle-aged and old people. For women as they age, the intersection of ageism with sexism can be devastating in circumscribing their activities and controlling their self-image. The varieties of ageism affecting women grow out of sex role stereotypes and discrimination combined with ideas about the nature of the middle-aged and old. Feminist critiques of sex role stereotypes and challenges to sexist claims about women's nature have not generally extended to old women; with few exceptions, feminists have failed to confront their own ageism or to challenge ageist constructions of the nature of women beyond midlife. The idea for this volume grew out of concerns expressed by members of the Task Force on Aging and Ageism of the National Women's Studies Association as we looked unsuccessfully in Women's Studies texts and classrooms for discussions of the last third of women's lives.

Women's Studies research and teaching respond to, and in turn inform, the agenda of the second wave of feminism where major issues have reflected for the most part young women's concerns: reproductive issues; female sexuality; child care; violence against women; equal opportunity in education and jobs; balancing careers and intimate relationships. It is time to round out the feminist agenda with issues of deep concern to women at midlife and beyond. Many of those issues are closely tied to the young women's

---

Evelyn R. Rosenthal, Associate Professor at the State University of New York at Binghamton's School of Education and Human Development, earned her PhD in sociology from Cornell. She has published on gender roles, schooling and women's work lives; at present, her research is focused on retired women workers. She co-founded the Women's Studies program at Binghamton and is a founding member of the National Women's Studies Association.

1

agenda that forms the core of struggle for second wave feminists; yet, research stops short of recognizing that these same core feminist issues continue to be concerns in the last third of women's lives. One aim of this book is to make explicit the implied connections of ageism and sexism by presenting research delineating the forms core feminist issues take in midlife and old age.

The concerns of younger women do not generally carry on into midlife and old age unmodified. The politics of reproduction, for example, are more likely to refocus away from control over childbirth toward the cessation of reproductive potential and women's challenge to a disease model of menopause. Issues of sexuality move toward exploring varieties of sexual expression available to women who inhabit in old age a largely single-sex social world. Concern with mitigating the social isolation experienced by women caring for children within a nuclear family structure shifts to concern for the social isolation of nuclear family spouses when one requires long term care or dies. Violence against women is not solely a young women's issue, although young women victims dominate our consciousness from media portrayals as well as from the self-censorship fearful middle-aged and old women apply to their own freedom of movement. The struggle for equal opportunity in education and jobs finds its parallel in pension reform lobbying, and the feminization of poverty is overwhelmingly the poverty of old women. And as young people embrace a dual-career family form, giving rise to an avalanche of advice and research about how to make it work, can they possibly believe that working it out in their twenties and thirties means they will not need to continue inventing it for the next thirty years through their retirement? Most feminists today would agree, I am confident, that our challenge to patriarchal constructions of women's nature has begun to make a difference in the way young women live their lives. It is time to accept a new challenge aimed at transforming older women's lives.

In extending feminist research to middle age and beyond, the essays in this book taken together comprise a critique of the conditions of the last third of women's lives. Each essay shows its debt to earlier feminist research in its use of analytic tools and methodologies developed and modified by feminists to explore questions previously unasked. The first contribution is an example of one of the earliest feminist modifications of research methods, that of letting the subjects of analysis speak for themselves. In it, Noreen Hale asks us to listen to seven of her friends tell us what it is like to be old. As the women describe specific losses and fears, we hear them question or accept events in their own lives. Whether or not the women express a critique of their personal condition in political terms, their stories present a prologue to subsequent essays that contribute to a critique of middle and old age in America.

Friendless isolation is no more natural to old age than it is to early motherhood, yet what many women fear about growing old is the isolation they perceive as inevitable. Middle-aged and old women need a critique of the naturalness of their isolation to break through ageist barriers that lead them to reject other old women as potential friends. Ruth Harriet Jacobs discovers the roots of older women's isolation in earlier sex role conditioning that led many to value men over women and emphasize family involvement to the exclusion of ongoing friendship formation with women outside the family. In her essay on "Friendships Among Old Women," Jacobs describes successful strategies for breaking out of friendless isolation and extends the feminist critique of women's proper place into old age.

With aging come changes in physical appearance, but those changes need not be dreaded as inevitable ugliness. Our need to pass as young or middle-aged reflects our ageism turned inward, but is complicated by our recognition of institutionalized ageism set to make economic survival more difficult for women who no longer appear young. Ann Gerike's discussion of gray hair as metaphor and manifestation of women's aging, "On Gray Hair and Oppressed Brains," reveals the contradictions we face if we choose to attempt passing or not. With her insight in mind, we can come to see similarities with the contradictions present in younger women's choices of self-presentation style.

Along with changes in appearance, aging brings internal changes as well; we are not merely young women wrinkled and gray. At the heart of ageism against women is our inevitable loss of reproductive capacity, often hastened by surgery. The effects of hysterectomy, powerfully analyzed by Dorin Schumacher in "Hidden Death: The Sexual Effects of Hysterectomy," relate to two areas at the core of young women's struggle: the control of childbirth and the under-

standing of women's sexuality. Schumacher applauds women's
gains in controlling their own experiences of childbirth and provides research to support women's need to control their own cessation of reproductive potential. She extends the feminist analysis of
the politics of reproduction into the last third of life. In addition, by
her research she moves us toward overcoming our lack of understanding of our own sexuality and our failure to prize it even as we
celebrate a new sexual freedom.

Women's success in gaining access to education and careers un-
derlies the modern buzz-words of "having it all" and leads feminists to support public policies designed to lighten the burden on
individual women attempting to integrate personal and professional
concerns. Most analyses of personal and professional integration
are undertaken within the confines of heterosexual marriage and
focus on child care, spousal role negotiation and early career flexibility, as if the integration will be accomplished in our thirties for a
lifetime; taking her own experiences as a starting point for "Love
and Work After 60" and the experiences of both a support group
and a therapy group for "We Are Not Your Mothers," Rachel Siegel
extends the analysis of balancing personal and professional life into
old age where she meets new challenges with few models to guide
her. Along the way, she critiques the positive stereotyping of successful old women by young colleagues who seem unwilling to allow us to be needy, dependent and weepy at times. She reminds us
that pedestals are confining no matter who the architect.

The challenges of a long-term marriage in the context of a feminist commitment to equality contrast sharply with the experiences
of spouses in traditional marriages. Sandra Quinn-Musgrove ex-
plores women's dilemma as wife/nurse giving extended care to a
dying husband. Women see no satisfactory way out of the increased
isolation they and their ailing spouses experience as illness lingers
for years. Most honor their commitment to selfless caregiving in
line with religious beliefs as well as sex role expectations; in one
case of rebellion, public censure is avoided by secrecy while self-
censure continues to be draining. None of the surviving spouses
interviewed here expresses a clear critique of her position and the
social policies that maintain it, and most learn with difficulty to
admit the anger they experience in doing what was expected of

them as wives. Quinn-Musgrove provides a tool to assist spouse/ caregivers in the tasks of admitting to anger and forgiving the self, and demonstrates its operation in her essay. Her analysis of social isolation and problematic return to life outside family relationships parallels earlier feminist analyses of the limits of the nuclear family and the effects on young mothers of the isolation of childcare.

None of the midlife lesbians in Barbara Sang's sample is concerned with finding an identity outside the confines of nuclear family life and traditional gender roles as most writing on midlife women stress; for this group of women, that task was accomplished earlier. Many in her sample are mothers, and several when younger were in heterosexual marriages; nevertheless, at midlife they are enjoying the results of successful professional lives, since traditional sex roles were rejected long ago. They look to their own adolescent life dreams for sources of creativity in integrating old and new aspects of the self at midlife. Sang's work underlines the variety of women's experience in midlife and extends past youth the feminist critique of a psychology that requires women's withdrawal into family life at young adulthood.

Women who manage to balance family life and careers in the context of heterosexual marriage often do so at great personal cost. Often, as Jacobs pointed out in her analysis of friendship, the cost is social isolation when widowed, since little time was devoted to developing friendship-building skills. The challenge of retirement poses different perils, according to Joy Reeves' analysis of dual-career families. Sources of strain shift to role-cycling dilemmas and identity problems as women move into a once-rejected role of full-time housewife and spouses pressure each other to retire simultaneously. Reeves' major point is that all we know of dual-career families is confined to young and mostly affluent examples. She outlines the questions we need to ask about this family form in its later stages before we can assess its general viability as well as its compatibility with feminist goals of maximizing women's opportunities and choices.

The interdependence of family life and creative life for women is a topic of speculation for Autumn Stanley in her historical investigation of a group of prolific women inventors, "Invention Begins At Forty: Older Women of the 19th Century as Inventors." By drawing our attention to the connection between year of first patent and year of birth for these women inventors, Stanley reveals middle-aged creativity as normative rather than exceptional. Her painstaking research successfully challenges popular stereotypes of the professional inventor as young and male, and more generally expands our vision of the possibilities of women's achievement in midlife and old age.

As is often the case, poets express insights ahead of the rest of us, but they are kind enough to leave a well-marked trail for those willing to learn to read the signals (as the poems contributed to this book by Ingrid Reti and Mira Spektor illustrate). In her review essay, "Inventing Freedom: The Positive Poetic 'Mutterings' of Older Women," Jo C. Searles gives old women poets their due for being trailblazers in the critique of ageism and sexism.

Varieties of ageism directed toward women today contribute to a picture of aging women as unproductive, dependent, rigid, weak, defenseless, morally old-fashioned, timid, ugly, senile, and lonely. The list of negative stereotypes can be extended, making it no surprise that younger women look past us and through us as if by denying our existence they will magically avoid growing old. Positive stereotypes harm us less directly but in the end are no less limiting, casting us as perfect mothers forbidden our own neediness, or wisdom-filled crones denied challenge and growth. Often, when one of us by our actions contradicts the stereotypes of the nature of old women, we are told we are exceptions or we are permitted to pass as young. Feminists whose analysis of sexism brilliantly and devastatingly changed ideas about the nature of women must recognize how a parallel analysis of ageism uncovers similar mechanisms at work constructing the nature of old age. By investigating the lives of old women we can challenge stereotypes, critique old age as a social construction, and discover that much of what we as women fear about our own aging is not natural to old age.

Being Old:
Seven Women, Seven Views

Noreen Hale, EdD

SUMMARY. Part of a larger study to ascertain learning needs elderly women experienced over their lifetimes, this essay describes firsthand what it is like to grow old in America today. Selected excerpts from the life histories of seven women communicate this perspective.

The idyllic "good old days" when old people led socially defined "productive" lives and found peace and security in the open arms and homes of adult children simply never existed. People often died "old" at 49. America's middle-aged population, sandwiched between two sets of responsibilities and problems related to children and parents has not retreated from these formidable demands. But, it is not always easy to be patient, caring, and empathic. They ask, "Why can't Mom be her 'old self?'" and "What can I expect when I'm her age?"

The middle-aged struggle with these issues as they attempt to come to grips with their parents' aging and, ultimately, their own. In any communication, we must first listen to what is being transmitted before we can respond. We need to hear what the elderly have to say to us about what it means to be old before we can answer their needs and ours relevantly and effectively.

By the quality of their lives the seven women interviewed defy

Noreen Hale is Director, Curriculum Development, National College of Education, Lombard, IL. Dr. Hale has teaching and work experience in the field of aging; the latter includes positions as Manager, Community Relations, MacNeal Hospital, Berwyn, IL; Consultant for Adult and Geriatric Programs, Tri-City Mental Health Center, East Chicago, IN; and Director, Continuing Education in Mental Health Care of the Aged (NIMH Grant), Columbus, IN.

stereotyping. From their worlds, we can sketch a portrait of today's American old women. They tell us who they are and what we may expect. They tell us of pain, joy, fear, hope. They tell us of shattered illusions, joyous discoveries, roadblocks to growth and creative adaptation. They tell us of reality.

The biographical excerpts provided here from the life histories of seven women are selections from transcripts of tapes dealing with one (i.e., "What it means to grow old") of nine question sets administered via structured and semi-structured interviews. The women became interviewees based on the recommendations of local clergy, of the author's friends, and of her colleagues who worked in nursing homes, community mental health centers, and area agencies on aging. Preliminary contacts were made with prospective subjects to explain the purpose and likely duration of the study and to gauge rapport between interviewer and interviewee. Each old woman was interviewed over a period of six months, averaging one to two visits a month; the "official" taped interview lasted one hour, but the author spent much of the day "visiting" with the women. A purely oral history approach was used at first to allow time for a trust relationship to develop between researcher and subject and, especially, for the women to gradually become accustomed to discussing progressively personal matters. The material contained in this essay has been edited to communicate the experience of women growing old in America today.

THIS IS WHO WE ARE: HEAR US

Margaret at 70: A "Lily of the Field"

A risk I took in my life that I am proud of is selling my home and moving to an apartment where I am living alone. It was hard because the house had so many happy memories. I think my only goal at this time is to live one day at a time and not to worry about what tomorrow brings. Like lilies of the field, life for me now is different inasmuch as I have slowed down considerably physically. However, I think the living process has made me mellow, and less afraid to deal with people, and to be more understanding of the needs of others.

I always wanted to die when I became 60. I always figured you still had your faculties, so 60 wasn't a bad age to go out. Above that it might be a little risky, but I'm glad to be hanging around at 70. I do think that, as you get older, you're able to deal with people a little more.

I think older people can still be very helpful. I think, for the most part, they are trying to get older people involved and invite them to come and do things, like here for our Oktoberfest. I was working in Connie's Place, a bar, selling tickets. Now a woman called me from the sodality and asked if I'd help with the clothes drive next week. . . . I've been playing piano at a Senior Center once a week. I've also played in a nursing home. I would like to do some candy-striping if my feet were better.

Life is very meaningful for me. I'm a great believer in afterlife and especially when they say you meet your loved ones. I'm not too anxious to carry on. I begin every day by going to Mass because I love to. I just stay closer to God that way. It's very important in my life. I think He has taken care of me so well 'cause I depend on Him. As my husband used to say, "Keep in good with the Big Boss."

Well, in a eulogy, maybe my daughter could say "she tried to brighten senior citizens' lives;" that might be a good one. I do make a lot of people happy when I get there, I think. Also, she could say that I had three wonderful girls, each uniquely special, and each one knows that she has a special place in my heart . . . and a lot of their friends have become my friends — like yourself, for instance. So if you want to say something in my eulogy, you can. You could mention, "She was a pretty good Joe — she liked me and I liked her."

Andrea at 76: Starting Over

I retired in 1972. I was living in an apartment by myself, and I did accounting on my own — enough to make what I needed. I had my stroke while I was out there. After I had it, I left the hospital and went to a convalescent center. There I took therapy. I had to learn to walk again. It didn't affect my speech, but it left this side partially paralyzed. So, I can't do much with this hand. I left the convalescent center because my insurance ran out. Then I went to live with a retired nurse. She helped me an awful lot. And she had a lovely collection of records. I think music helps an awful lot; it was classical. She really helped me more than anybody.

I transferred my church membership here when I moved into this nursing home. And I'm glad I did because that's a good way to get acquainted with people. The feeling I miss is when I go out and don't see anybody I know. I don't get over to Fort Wayne much anymore. The friend who used to come after me has muscular dystrophy, and it's getting hard for her to walk, and she'd been so nice to me.

My friends came over here. In September we had a picnic, and they correspond with me all the time. I get a lot of mail. Another friend's getting rid of her things now. Sooner or later we all have to do it. Now my things are scattered.

Well, I'm trying to write, you know. I haven't had anything published, but I took a test, a writer's test and they told me I had ability so I guess I'll just keep plugging away. I wrote about life in the nursing home here, and I'm trying to send it around to get published. I'm working now on the photos. I've got two more pictures on the film to go.

I think that most people at age 70 would like to still be out in public and involved with people and activities. I would like to make some money rather than to depend on the government totally—it's so expensive here. And, more than that, I want to keep my mind active—I don't want to "dry up" as a person.

Clara at 79: Looking Ahead

I don't pry into anybody's business. I was taught whatever anybody told me to keep my mouth shut. So, I do that. As I was taught, other people's worries are worse than yours. And if they came around you for advice, listen and console them . . . but don't burden them with yours. So I never did. I talk more now—since I met all these other people who keep asking me questions!

The only difference I see with age is that I was strong and healthy when I was young. I can't do the things I used to do now and that irks me. I wouldn't say there was any drastic change—it just came

normally. Then, I haven't been able to go to my daughter out west for the last two years because I'm not well enough to travel.

All I want is to be financially comfortable and to be in good enough health to travel. In 1918 influenza settled in my ears. In 1963, they found the perforated left ear, and in 1965 they found "another hole in my head" — so I can't travel. When I could go by train, I could walk back and forth, but on the bus, I can't move. I tried to fly, but the higher I go the worse it is. So, they have to help me down the ramp and just put me on the plane in St. Louis. It took me four days to get over it. So, I can't fly and I can't take the bus 'cause I get too cramped, and I don't know how to drive. So, I haven't been there since 1976. My daughter was here last year. Now, if I could go with somebody, every so often we could stop. But a lot of people I felt I could call on are all gone. They either moved away or died.

As far as my own death, I'm not afraid. If it's my time, it's my time. It doesn't worry me. I believe there's an afterlife. So I don't worry about it; it's going to be better anyway.

A gift I'd like to leave the next generation is my gift of psychic reading. I'd like to come back next generation and be a guardian angel to somebody and go ahead with my work. I know there's an afterlife — I'm not worried about that — but I'd want to be allowed to come back to help someone advance himself or herself in their psychic work.

The three things I'd like to be remembered for? One thing that comes to mind is to remember me as I am. In other words, accept me — when I'm in a good humor, bad humor, or whatever. Then I would say I'd like to be remembered for my psychic work. And then third — I don't know what to say — I don't want people to think I'm boasting. Well, I guess the third thing would be the love I give to the world.

Harriet at 81: Individualism in an Institution

My health was very good until my late 70s. Then many things happened. My blood pressure got up to 260, and I was on my feet working at the store. . . . I had a heart attack and cancer surgery at age 69 with complete recovery. I never worried much over that. And Tom was also having many illnesses, and from then on that's all it was. He died at 79. We knew he was dying; there was no regret—I mean, it was a time that had come. He couldn't get well; he had emphysema so bad, and one bout of pneumonia after another.

We'd run out of insurance. He'd been in so much they wouldn't take him anymore. He was moved to the VA hospital, was there 12 days and died. We both knew when we parted that was it. I can't explain it—I accepted that. I haven't grieved over him. In fact, I told somebody, "we couldn't afford for Tom to live."

In my 60s, I said many times when I get old if I have pleasant surroundings, compatible friends, and don't have to worry too much about finances—I'll be content. Now at 81, I have all three. But if inflation keeps up, I don't know about the finances. So, my oldest son says he will stand by when that time comes. I'm still loved. I have been all my life. Once in a while I feel a little neglected—my friends are all getting old so they don't come and see me and take me out like I wish they would. But they have their problems, too.

Honey, I can just adjust . . . why, people here just carry on so. I knew when I came to the nursing home I was going to have to live here. I burned all my bridges behind me. I've liked it and I think it's the way for old people to live.

I don't want to be senile or a vegetable. Even if I don't become senile, I don't want to live too much longer, I really don't. I'm going to be having financial problems even if Bud says he'll step in. My two bills this month came to $834, room and board and drug bill. I don't have that much income.

Right now, I'm still doing volunteer work. At 81, I'm still writing two articles monthly for the *News Daily* on our activities at the home, and I'm on the Resident Council, serving as greeting chairman to the newcomers.

You don't want things for yourself so much like I used to want things so much for my pretty home. You just don't desire things so much. Every once in a while if I see a picture of New England, I think I'd like to go there again, but then I laugh to myself, "Why, it wears me out to go to the dining room."

There's more religion watching the "Waltons" than all the Bible reading in the world, or with some of these old people being kind to one another. The other morning this 93-year-old man, Ben, came leading a blind man in to breakfast. I said to Linda, "Isn't that beautiful?" and Linda started to cry. But I see religion in all this. And I see God in nature, and I can remember my granddaughter saying when we were outside walking, "Grandma, I don't believe like they tell it in church. I like to come out here and look up in the sky and think that God's up there looking down."

Nancy at 74: Gentle Realist

Two crises for us have been my husband's precarious health over a period of nearly 30 years and this serious coronary last April. I live only one day at a time. Also, my husband's retirement because, I don't care who you are, you make some adjustments. Mine did not retire as early as some.

The fact that I had to be on my own so much—he always had a job where he was gone a great deal—made it difficult to adjust. And you have to handle everything as it comes up by yourself, and you don't realize that you've been doing those things on your own for so long. Without asking anybody you made these decisions, and here he is, and he wants to take over some of those things. And it does make for problems. You've been by yourself all day and done what you wanted to do when you wanted to do it.

My first goal now is to take care of him and to take care of the grandchildren and to contribute something to other people. I'm still active in church. I notice now that I represent the senior citizens on committees and things of that sort. Nobody told me that, but it's easy to see. It was an awful shock to me the first time I looked around a committee and found out I was the oldest one there. But it doesn't bother me now. I'm glad I can represent that point of view. But I miss contact with younger people; I don't have as much of that as I would like.

I have to admit that at 74 I'm elderly. But I don't feel any different, I don't think, from what I did at 64. The thing that was hardest for me to take was when the younger people would help me up steps and things like that I didn't feel I needed or would show such deference to me. It really got to me! I'm beginning to just ignore it and take it and just go on. I'll admit it was hard for me to take.

One thing that's important to the elderly is to be "alive" as long as they live 'cause that's the specter that haunts most old people, I think. They don't mind dying, but that "existence." We gave our family doctors explicit directions that we don't want to be kept in a state of living death. Jason and I have talked it over and we don't want extreme measures taken to resuscitate either one of us.

I think I've had a good life, and I think we need to move on and leave it to somebody else. I think it might get boring if we lived very long. You'd start to think, "Well, I've been here before." And I'm not sure I'd do anything any better if I went on than I have in the past. No, I wouldn't want to live my life over.

Today, often, it doesn't seem as if we have much direction—except from the study of history. I consider myself a link in the chain of human life. I hope I have strengthened the chain instead of weakening it. I have a great sense of history and the continuity of families and nations and so forth. I think that what we are today is affected by what's happened in the past, and what's going to happen in the future is affected by what we're doing and being today.

Ruth at 77: Taxing Transition

Some women grieve for their husbands terribly, and I tried to say to a couple of them, "Try to think of it that in a way they're really not dead." Surely they're not. I said, "Think of the nice things, think of all the happy times you had, think that we all are born and we start dying from the day we're born." I feel if you grieve after a person, you can't turn loose of them. It's not fair; it's not right. Sure I get angry sometimes that Paul had to go away and leave right when we could have been the happiest. It doesn't last very long, but I just get real angry.

I promised myself if I ever had grandchildren that they would remember me and they certainly do! There are five of them—one right after the other. And I used to go over there every time one was born and stay about six weeks. And I kept doing that when one would come along about every two years. I'd tell 'em stories. There were so many children and so much to do that Donna didn't get

much time to spend with each one of them. So, I would go in their bedroom — there were just three boys for a long time and they had little roll-a-beds — and we'd get down and tell stories.

In the last three years my health's been deteriorating pretty badly. I've been having heart monitors and cardiograms and had a cancer removed off my nose, and I was so nervous and my blood pressure was up. I'm on four different kinds of medication and it costs a fortune.

Well, I never thought that I would be quite so crippled up so early in life. I thought 65 was early in life to be crippled up, and I tried everything under the sun to get to feeling better so I could work. And I did work — but I pushed myself. Now, I just live from day to day because it isn't necessary I worry about what I'm going to do. The thing of it is I just hope I feel well enough to do the things I *have* to do.

I don't have anything to be absorbed in. I wish I did. But there's nothing I can get "into" at the present time. I doubt if I ever will because I can stay out an hour and a half or two hours; then I have to come home and rest.

I don't know how people feel about birth and death and tragedy, but to me, God never gave you too much that you can't stand it. And you cope with it. I was never a person to cry — I cry now, but I never used to. It's just the last year, but not too often. I think sometimes I bottled all my worries and all of my suffering inside and it just broke loose lately, about a year ago.

I often wondered what I was put here for. Maybe I haven't finished it. I think you stay until you've finished it, but I don't know what it is. My father used to sit out there in the shade and he'd say to me, "Wonder what I was put here for, Ruthie. Well, just being a good dad and a good grandfather and being happy. You've been happy most of your life, although it's been hard." Oh, we lived through terrible times in '29. I tell you, it was hard — 33 cents an hour. Nobody else had it. A lot of 'em was working on this WPA. But he never was out of a job — and he was real happy with it. So I said, "I guess that was your purpose — you brought four children into the world and we've all taken care of ourselves and that must have been one of them." He died when he was 92. He never suffered one thing, he just lay down and went to sleep. He was old and slow, but never suffered.

Elizabeth at 70: Concern and Commitment

I retired from teaching at age 63. They threw out Latin and me with it. I still have a license in French and English, but they wanted only spoken French taught and I was not good at that. I hadn't learned it that way, and I couldn't persuade them to try anything else. On Friday, the last day I was working, I was worth $14,000 a year, and by Monday I wasn't worth a plug nickel. That's a completely illogical system.

I think I'm finally getting to the place where I am considering a retirement home. My friends have made some deposits on retirement homes, and I think that might be a good idea since I'm a single person. I didn't have the money to do it when I retired. I thought, "Yikes, what am I going to do?" I thought I saved, but with inflation, you think you've saved enough and you suddenly find you haven't.

I am active as a precinct committeewoman. I'm going to file February 6 for that job again and for delegate to the State Convention. I was a delegate to the National Convention four years ago, and I might try that again.

I must admit I've been kind of semi-depressed for the last year and a half—being an environmentalist, I hate to see trees chopped down and little animals killed. But I have to keep reading between the lines and see there are good things going on too. I just have to concentrate on them.

Currently, I'm trying to use my religion; for example, you're always taught you can't change anybody's thinking but your own. So my idea is if God created man in His image and likeness then each person is created well spiritually, and it's my job to see God's influence in him and to look for the God-like qualities. . . .

I was thinking as I was reading through these questions, I was thinking as you get older there aren't so many hills and valleys, it's more level. The valleys are not so deep, and the hills are not so high. There are little pleasures like going with someone to the ball game in Cincinnati on a senior trip or something.

My own death doesn't bother me, but the loss of companionship of a friend, that was really difficult to accept. I'm kind of an independent person. I go a lot of places just by myself, but, nevertheless, it's lots more fun to go with someone. But younger "acquaintances" can't really replace old friends because you haven't shared the same experiences. There are certain pieces of time we can't discuss because we don't have them in common. To have a friend, you must be one. I don't know whether I have acquaintances or friends. After my mother died, I relied a lot on a good friend, but she died. So I don't really have anybody. I whisper in my dog's or cat's ear, I guess. I just whispered in yours.

Friendships Among Old Women

Ruth Harriet Jacobs, PhD

SUMMARY. Because of widowhood, divorce, retirement, and prejudice against them, old women are in special need of friendships with other women. Old women's friendships have many valuable functions. It is dangerous to depend on just one friend. There are impediments to making friendships in old age including projection of negativity about aging on other old women, lack of resources and transportation, fears of loss, invasion of privacy, obligations, and preference for males. Some women settle for paid therapists as friends or for self help groups. Communities can provide activities fostering friendships, and women themselves can learn how to make connections.

Alice, a sixty-year-old woman who had been divorced ten years ago, remarries. Selma, a close friend, who was divorced about the same time and met Alice shortly thereafter, provides, as a wedding gift, the expensive flowers for the wedding reception. Selma is not rich, but she wants her friend to have a beautiful wedding. However, she has ambivalent feelings, and she finds herself crying after the wedding.

Selma is a heterosexual woman who is glad that her friend has found a new husband. But that man lives in a distant state, and the couple has decided to live in his home. Selma knows that she will seldom see Alice and that Alice will be unavailable now for the trips they had been taking. Selma, after the pain of her divorce, had

---

Ruth Harriet Jacobs, a sociologist and gerontologist, retired recently as Chair of the Sociology Department at Clark University, and teaches part time at several Massachusetts colleges. She is a Visiting Research Scholar at the Wellesley College Center for Research on Women. She thanks the Stone Center for Developmental Services and Studies at Wellesley College for the grant to study depression-coping strategies of old women. This research provided data for this paper.

19

invested in the friendship with Alice and fears it will be difficult to replace her best friend. She doubts that she, herself, will remarry. She is probably right.

Many old women these days become divorced and are less apt to remarry than men, who remarry, on the average, younger women. In addition, widows predominate among old women because men die on the average seven years younger than women and have married women four years younger than themselves. By age 65 half of American women are widowed. After 65 there are two million United States widowers and eleven million widows. Friendships are thus more important to old women than to men who are usually married until death.

The still married woman has friendships with other couples plus, one hopes, the friendship with her mate. The never married woman already has her friendships and adjustments. Newly single women need friends badly, but most report that their still married friends are not forthcoming because of what I have called the Noah's Ark Syndrome in my poetic drama, *Button, Button, Who Has the Button?*

> They are still coming
> two by two off the ark.
> Hostesses do not invite
> unescorted single women
> divorcees or even widows
> expecting they will rape
> husbands, steal homes, or,
> worst trauma of all, mean
> an odd number at table.

Formerly married old women are frequently unwilling to go to events or activities alone. Even going solo to a movie, certainly not an interactive event, terrifies them. To take a trip alone seems an admission of being strange or is frightening. Many do not know how to make new friends.

Close women friends are important to most women through life, and women are more self-revealing in general to their friends than men. For many men, the wife is the confidant and friend, but many women seem to need and have relationships with women confidants. In fact, the sixty-year-old bride mentioned at the beginning of this article discovered that when she moved to her new residence with her new husband, she greatly missed her women friends. Living in a large city, she found it hard to find new friends and even went so far as to put notices up looking for women to play bridge, chess, or Scrabble as a way of meeting same-gender companions. She was happy in her marriage but found herself mourning her women friends and spent money frequently on long distance calls and trips to her former residence area.

The gender differences in friendship patterns through life were reviewed by gerontologist Beth B. Hess (1979). She found that "in old age, it appears that the interpersonal skills of women are highly functional, allowing them greater flexibility in the construction of social networks than is the case for old men." I agree that women often do have the skills for making new relationships but have also found that it is very difficult for some women in their sixties, seventies, eighties, and nineties to replace losses in their lives. While those who are mobile and have resources often do find new friends who sustain them and provide companionship, others are restricted by lack of transportation and money, by their own fears of involvement, their selectivity, and the discrimination against aged women.

Recently, I gave a talk at a meeting on mothers and daughters sponsored by the Wellesley College Center for Research on Women where I am a research scholar. After it, a woman about 70 years old came up and asked if I knew where she could meet bright women her age. She said, "Wherever I go these days, I seem to be the oldest woman in the room, and while people are polite to me, they do not seem interested in developing friendships. I find myself quite lonely, and I thought you might have some ideas for me."

Singles groups and services of all kinds exist for meeting cross-gender partners. There are also dating services for lesbian women, but non-lesbian women who want to meet compatible women often have difficulty if they move to new areas, lose old friends or spouses, or retire from jobs which had provided interaction.

Some old women can be alone but not lonely; others become depressed if they do not see people on a regular basis. If they do not have friends to buffer the relationship with their adult children, they may expect more time and attention from the children than the adult children can comfortably give. With the aid of a grant from the Stone Center for Developmental Services and Studies at Wellesley College, I have been studying ways that old women cope with depression. They have many strategies, but one important one is to get support from friends or to forget themselves and their problems and gain self esteem by giving to friends.

Sadly, when losses of friends occur through death or for other reasons, many old women find it hard to use available opportunities for making connections. It is difficult to persuade some women to go to events at senior centers and similar places where they will find age peers. This is because many women fear aging, deny their own aging, and project their hate of their aging upon other old women. They see other women as old but themselves as somehow different. When I studied a home for the aged, almost all the women on one floor rejected the other women. All said things like "They are all old and senile and stupid. They belong here; I don't. I am different. I am only here because of bad luck, bad children, bad housing, et cetera."

In the midst of people who could become friends, these women clung to an identity as different because they found it so hard to admit they were old. This is not surprising in view of the negative stereotypes this society has of old women. The stereotypes are internalized by many old women.

On the other hand, there are certainly plenty of environments for the elderly, including housing projects, where old women have reached out and made new friends and community. Sometimes this is because natural leaders and outgoing women make the effort and other times it is because of planned intervention by professionals.

To help old women make new friends, as well as to learn the skills for coping with practical problems of various sorts, I began some years ago to do workshops for old women. In these, they learned how to deal with aging, develop positive attitudes, survival strategies, have new activities, and make new friends in the group. To make it possible for women around the country to be in groups, self help or leader led, I wrote *Older Women Surviving and Thriving* (1987). This provides instructions and handouts for twelve sessions.

It is proving useful for women to be in these groups. Women also make friends in such organizations as Older Women's League chapters throughout the country, the Gray Panthers, and many local organizations for old people and intergenerational organizations.

Certain women have to be coaxed to venture. Not only are they afraid of loss again, but realistically many women have learned that friendship at older ages may sometimes become a burden. If the friend is more frail or becomes sick or needy in other ways, the woman who is stronger may have to deal with giving help, worrying, and taking responsibility. There is also fear that friends will want too much time and intimacy and encroach upon independence and individuality.

Many women who live in housing for the elderly have told me that they have made a strong commitment "not to get involved" with neighbors because they fear that they will not be able to get away from them. As one put it, "I am always friendly when I see people in the corridors but I am very careful not to invite people into my apartment or to accept invitations. I can't afford to move anyplace else, and I am afraid of starting to be close to someone here and then having no privacy at all." Another said, "Most people here no longer drive and I do. I don't want to become the building chauffeur."

My manual, described above, has been very useful in many settings, but one social worker who tried to use it in a very small elderly apartment building found that the women were not interested in getting to know one another. This was very sad because this building was in a "company town" to which these women had moved in old age to be near children who worked for a large corporation. They were quite lonely and dependent upon their children for companionship and really needed friends. Yet, they were terrified of the closeness of their neighbors, having formerly lived in single family houses.

Many old women would like to have friends of all ages and resent well-intentioned efforts to direct them toward their peers. They see this as ghettoization and stigmatization and even infantilization because of the types of planned events like Bingo.

It is urgent that communities provide places where old women, and old men for that matter, can come together on the basis of interests rather than age. Some towns and cities are fortunate to have indoor, year-round swimming pools, where in the intimacy of the locker room women can meet others and perhaps go out to lunch and develop friendships. Finding companions is a latent function of interesting activities for the kind of women who would never be caught going to a senior center. For example, in 1988 I obtained a small grant from the Massachusetts Arts Lottery Council, administered through Wellesley Town Arts Council, to teach four sessions of poetry writing to people over age 60. Twenty women and no men showed up even though the program was open to both genders. We had a marvelous time getting to know each other through sharing our poetry. Women in the class began to value each other greatly. Although the course was sponsored by the Wellesley Council on Aging, most of the participants in the class had not before that set foot into any Council on Aging programs. They needed to be brought in by a program that appealed to them as creative people, rather than simply elders.

People past sixty have found friends at Elderhostels, which are programs set up to bring elders to colleges and conference centers. These offer an inexpensive week-long package of food, housing, three courses, and sociability. Many old women start lasting friendships at them. I have been teaching Elderhostels for several years, principally at the Rowe Conference Center in Rowe, Massachusetts and Regis College in Weston, Massachusetts. At hostels, women alone outnumber the couples largely because women live longer and there are more of them. I am pleased that women in my Elderhostels have made friends and gone to visit each other afterwards.

I remember one woman who had just been divorced and had come to the Elderhostel hoping to meet a man. At the first breakfast, she left the table abruptly, and I followed, concerned. Her eyes were full of tears. I asked, "What is the matter?"

She replied, "A man at my table got up to get his wife a cup of coffee. It made me feel terrible because I have nobody now to do anything for me and care for me." I pointed out that there were other women at the Elderhostel who were widowed, divorced, or never married. She said, "I don't care. I am not interested in being with women." Her demeanor was very angry.

Some women have not been accustomed to female friendships because husbands, children, or work have taken up their lives. They need to learn in old age how to enjoy the companionship of other women and not value only men, which some were taught to do as girls. Men are indeed in short supply at later ages, and old women are marvelous. I was pleased to see that with a little nudging on my part, this woman began to associate with other women at the Elderhostel. By the end of the week, she had made friends and was feeling better about herself and life.

A segment of old women for the first time in later years express their sexuality with women partners. This may be because of the unavailability of men, but it also may be because same-sex partners provide great satisfaction. Some who have followed convention may be women who have suppressed lesbianism earlier to accommodate to society. But others may find attraction to women a new phenomena. Sexuality may be expressed physically or it may be sublimated in various ways.

For *Older Women Surviving and Thriving* I planned to write for the session on sexuality and family relations a few vignettes on ways old women express sexuality. However, I found I had to do a whole alphabet from Anne to Zena because so many variations exist. Here are three items from the "Alphabet of Ways of Expressing Sexuality for Old Women."

"Dorothy has been a lesbian all of her life, and she continues to have a sexual relationship with the woman who has been her lifetime partner."

"Evelyn, in younger years, had relationships with men. Now she meets few available men, and she satisfies her sexual needs with other women."

"Frieda is close to her women friends and shares good and bad times with them. But she does not have sexual relationships with them and would not consider this, although she finds it nice to touch and hug her women friends. They all enjoy the human warmth and comforting."

On the other hand, some old women have complained that bright and interesting women with whom they would like to be friends are lesbians. They are uncomfortable with them because they are afraid of social stigma or unwanted physical relationships. Old lesbian women who are part of the lesbian culture have a set of friends, but other aged lesbians are in situations where they experience extreme isolation if they have lost partners, have not come out, or lack friends or community.

The data tell us that women who are no longer young, regardless of various sexual preferences, are the largest consumers of counseling and therapy from individual clinicians and social agencies. It is hypothesized that this is because women can express their feelings more openly and also feel less stigmatized than men in seeking and getting professional help. I believe that often therapy is a substitute for friendships. The therapist becomes a paid friend, less threatening than a friend who might require reciprocity or who could prove unpredictable or problematic. The therapist, though costly, must take care of the emotional needs of the client without expecting emotional support in return. There is a safety in this. The therapist relationship may also be terminated without guilt. A friendship relationship which becomes undesired cannot usually be terminated without hurting the other person. There can be expectations that the therapist will change one's life for the better, something that is a great deal to expect of friends or for friends to deliver.

For these and other reasons, many mid-life and old women remain in long term relationships with therapists or have a series of therapeutic encounters as an antidote to loneliness. Others seek out self help groups such as Alcoholics Anonymous, Overeaters Anonymous, Al Anon, Emotions Anonymous, etc. I have studied these groups and discovered that some people in them really do not have the condition which the group treats. When I questioned one woman in Adult Children of Alcoholics who had had no alcoholic parents or intimates, she explained, "Well, my family was really dysfunctional like alcoholic families. I find the meetings very useful. It is nice to have some place to go."

Overeaters Anonymous members include women whose main problem is loneliness, not food, though, of course, O.A. also serves those with food disorders. Women make a life out of going to meetings every night. They do not have to be alone. Still, they never have to develop individual friendships, as many of their social needs are met in the group meetings. They can hear revelations and they can reveal, but it is confined to the ritualized hour or two of the meetings. Though many women do make friends whom they see outside of such groups, others can elect interaction within the structure only. They can telephone sponsors every day as a free service to control their eating. This provides sustained and routinized daily contact with a nurturer. Yet, they are not entangled in a web of reciprocity that extends to other aspects of their lives.

Some years ago I attempted to explain the proliferation of emotive and control groups in this society. Partly, it is out of our pervasive anxiety and alienation and partly out of our utopianism. Such groups provide time- and space-bound utopian communities in which people seek acceptance and perfectibility. In their functions, these groups are like the full-time utopian communities which flourished in the nineteenth century and again, briefly, during the late 1960s and early seventies.

For the friendless or friend-seeking, self help groups which now proliferate in our rather unhappy society provide a part-time sense of belonging, hope, interaction, and relief from the terrors of isolation. They are a surrogate community in a society characterized in many places by an absence of community and by relationships which are impersonal and exploitative rather than close and comforting.

Is it surprising that old women who have had losses and discontinuities in their lives seek out such groups? In mainstream organizations and settings, old women often experience prejudiced rejection. In most self help groups, they are welcomed and made to feel important. As I wrote in *Life After Youth: Female, Forty. What Next?* (1979) some old women alone become perpetual or temporary seekers looking for groups that will supply needs which other people meet in their work, family, and friendship networks.

It is important to point out that despite the needy women I have been discussing, many old women are embedded in deeply satisfying friendships and friendship networks. In fact, in *Life After Youth: Female, Forty. What Next?* one of the ten types of women I described from my research were women I called chum networkers. These might have family or work, volunteer or paid, but their chief satisfaction came from relationships with friends. Women are generally characterized by what psychiatrist Jean Baker Miller and the others at the Stone Center for Developmental Studies and Services at Wellesley College call the self in connectedness or relationship, rather than an isolated self. Miller and colleagues see this characteristic of women as positive, not as weakness or dependence. They suggest, as Miller does in *Toward a New Psychology of Women* (1977) that this is a better model for humanity than the independent macho male model.

After their children have grown and their husbands experience the earlier mortality of men, old women are often sustained by friendships developed over the years and by new ones made in later life. Being divorced, with children 34 and 37, I know personally, as well as through research, how vital are the friendships which embrace us in our hours of certainty and in times of uncertainty. I am grateful for my friends, and I wish to make more of them as I move on from 64. I know from my research and from my experience that it is foolish to invest in only one friendship, especially in later years. Many women like to have a best friend, but if other friendships are neglected, we are at risk in our later years, given our mortality, our moves and our moods.

It is important to have a number of friends who are available for different activities. Younger friends are insurance, while older ones can teach us what is to come. We need to emulate those old women who are remarkable in their capacity for broadening their horizons and their selves by reaching out to new people. Even if friendships are transitory, they enrich and develop us. Our development and growth continues through life. In old age, as in younger years, we need short or long term friends to confirm our identity, our importance, our connectedness to others, to be there in our time of need, and even just plain to fill our hours.

In a world largely hostile to old women, their friendships can be a buffer and a triumph of solidarity and support. Old women, rich in friendships, can help their daughters, granddaughters, and great granddaughters look forward to the fullness of old womanhood instead of dreading it. We old women can weep with our friends as necessary, but we can also laugh with them. As a contribution to our laughter, I offer some doggerel about women's friendships.

1.

Having friends after fifty
can be really nifty
since hotel rates are shifty
being similar for one or two

and you also can get blue
if waiters say "just one"
seat you in the blinding sun,
give you a stale single bun
and make you want to run.

2.

Taking a friend at six 0
is a good way to go
to a course on psych or Poe
or learn how easily to hoe
the older woman's row
in a class where you unload
righteous anger at a toad
who demeaned and mocked you
and other older women too.

3.

At seventy or seventy plus
friends make a welcome fuss
if you are well or sadly ill.
They sweeten almost any pill.
Friends will quickly share
a joy, a loss. They care.
Your friends swap jokes,
tales of old folks,
admire your clothes and kids
and unscrew tough jar lids.

4.

At eighty, women friends
visit while your hip mends,
ask you for advice
or what is really nice
or how to get rid of mice
and how much of a spice,
and graciously repeat twice.
If you can no longer drive,

they will see you thrive
by taking you out until five.

5.

At ninety or even more
friends come to your door
to learn about old days
and earlier women's ways.
They know it really pays
to understand how each phase
of a woman's life has niches
that only the great riches
of women's friendships fill,
in youth and when over the hill.

To make possible the riches of old women's friendships, both society and individuals must make sustained efforts. Communities and the organizations within them, including religious ones, can foster old women's friendships by providing settings and activities in which they may blossom. Educational institutions can help by offering courses, workshops, and activities for old women, such as those at the splendid Prime Time Women's Resource Center at the University of Richmond in Virginia or Boston University's Evergreen College. Arts Councils can fund old women's writing workshops and workshops like the ones I do. Other opportunities can be developed.

Individuals can also be tutored in the friend-making process. As a contribution to this, I conclude with some of my suggestions that women have found useful.

1. Go more than half way to make friends. Other women are lonely and shy too, even though they don't seem to be on the surface.
2. Read your local paper and bulletin boards carefully and go to meetings, events, gatherings that interest you. It will be there that you find women with your interests. Don't think you can make friends sitting at home.
3. If there is a movie or some event you want to attend, call up a woman you'd like to know better and invite her. She may be

grateful, but if she can't attend, don't be rebuffed. She may have another plan. Try again. People are grateful if you plan outings and reach out.

4. If you move to a new neighborhood, volunteer to canvass for the United Fund or some other cause. It is a good way to meet your neighbors. Also, ask your reference librarian for a list of local organizations.

5. If you attend church or a temple, during the coffee hour go up to women you'd like to meet. Extend yourself. Serve on committees. Attend social events sponsored by your religious denominations.

6. Take a course. Many are free for those over 60. Use whatever women's organizations and networks exist in your geographic area.

7. Organize a potluck supper for women you have met. Maybe they'll become frequent events.

8. Don't limit yourself to women your age. You can mentor younger women. You can learn from older women in preparation for your own aging.

9. Do volunteer work or serve on committees. Get involved in causes. You'll meet friends that way.

10. If you have been hurt by a friend, realize that you may have misunderstood, or misperceived, or your friend may have been hurt by you, though it was unintentional. Talk things out with that friend.

11. Join your local chapter of the Older Women's League or start a chapter. The national address: 730 Eleventh Street, N.W., Suite 300, Washington, DC 20001.

12. If you are a widow, call the Council on Aging or Senior Center in your town to find out where there is a widow's program you can attend. You will get help and make new friends.

13. Join an Older Women Surviving and Thriving Workshop. If there isn't one in your area, get the manual by that title at $17.95, plus $2.50 mailing, from Family Service America, 11700 West Lake Park Drive, Milwaukee, WI, or from the author, Ruth Harriet Jacobs, 75 High Ledge Avenue, Wellesley, MA 02181. You'll get help with your problems and meet

new friends. The manual will tell you how to find other women for the group and how to do 12 sessions.

14. At a meeting space at a church, temple, community center, etc. start a support group for old women of some other kind than mentioned in #13 above.

15. Join or start a Great Books group at your library.

16. See what is going on at the nearest senior center. Don't reject your aging or be snobbish about your age. Old women are great.

17. Develop a variety of friends for different activities. It is dangerous to limit yourself to one best friend because of mobility, mortality, and other reasons that could bring loss.

18. Consider shared living arrangements. Look into them with other women.

19. Realize that lack of privacy or having to provide reciprocity is less dangerous than isolation.

20. Realize that you will get along better with your adult children if you have a busy, happy life with friends than if you are dependent upon your children for companionship. Your adult children will like you better if you are not demanding. You will give your daughter a gift of not fearing her own old womanhood if you are occupied with friends and activities.

21. Don't wait for an absolutely perfect friend. Nobody is perfect. Not even you!

REFERENCES

Hess, Beth. (1979). Sex Roles, Friendship and the Life Course. *Research on Aging, 1*, 494-515.

Jacobs, Ruth Harriet. (1971). The Emotive and Control Groups As New Mutated Utopian Communities. *Journal of Applied Behavioral Science*, 7, 234-251.

Jacobs, Ruth Harriet. (1979). *Life After Youth: Female, Forty. What Next?* Boston: Beacon Press.

Jacobs, Ruth Harriet. (1987). *Older Women Surviving and Thriving: A Manual for Group Leaders*. Milwaukee: Family Service America.

Jacobs, Ruth Harriet. (1988). *Button, Button, Who Has the Button?* Durham, N.C.: Crones Own Press.

Miller, Jean Baker. (1977). *Toward a New Psychology of Women*. Boston: Beacon Press.

Untitled

I know why you are afraid to touch
the other woman here in the room.
She is heavier than she used to be,
her hair is greyer,
her make-up heavier.
There is an unforeseen small hump
on the back of her neck,
her breasts are a bit lumpy —
She wears bright prints
with a vengeance,
she laughs and argues
at too high a volume.
She can't lift luggage
or wriggling children;
she can't bend down or bow
to pain and other time-wasters.
She repeats herself and forgets
some details that glue her days.
Are her late adventures grotesque,
her art an outdated song?
She insists on remembering
old patterns and stories —
She can't decently hide love
and heat and really, at her age,
that can't be passion!
Her perfume is too strong,
her skin too spongy-soft —
her teeth might emit a smell,
her smile an untold censure.
You would never wear clothes like that
or move through the day like that.

Thank God, since you're both so busy,
you can forget about each other—
And you never need to hug,
when you both reach out an arm
and a hand, and feel
a mirror.

—Mira Josefowitz Spektor
262 Central Park West
New York, NY 10024

On Gray Hair and Oppressed Brains

Ann E. Gerike, PhD

SUMMARY. After presenting factual information about the graying of hair, this article focuses on the connections between ageism, sexism, and women's dyeing of their gray hair, a subject seldom addressed by feminists. Sexual, social, and economic pressures to color hair and deny age are described, as are indications that attitudes toward gray hair are slowly beginning to change. The political and personal advantages of graying naturally are discussed.

Gray hair is universally viewed as an indication of advancing age, though the age at which hair begins to gray varies widely among individuals. Changes in hair color begin sooner than most people realize. A study of Australian blood donors in 1965, for example, revealed that, by the time they were twenty-five, 22 to 29 percent of the men in the group and 23 to 35 percent of the women had some obvious graying (Parachini, 1987). The age at which people begin to gray seems to be genetically determined, as are the graying patterns.

Much of the gray effect is produced by the mixture of light and dark hairs, though as dark hair loses its color it is genuinely gray for a time. Blond hair, of course, "grays" much less noticeably than darker hair. The proportion of white to dark hairs has to be well over 50 percent before it begins to show decisively.

Little research has been done on the graying of hair, so most of

Ann E. Gerike is a licensed consulting psychologist in the state of Minnesota. She works with the Creative Aging program at Pyramid Mental Health Center, with an employee assistance program, and has a private practice as a therapist. Since 1986 she has been the Convenor of the Aging and Ageism Caucus of NWSA. Address requests for copies to: 3215 Columbus Ave. S., Minneapolis, MN 55407.

what is known about it is assumption and guesswork. But the basic process appears to be the following:

> Each of the 100,000 hairs on the head is controlled by a hair bulb below the follicle at the deepest part of the root system. It is through the hair bulb that a variety of complex substances are channeled, creating each hair, mainly composed of a bio-chemical substance called keratin.
>
> In the hair roots and in the epidermis, millions of protein-producing pigment cells, called melanocytes, produce chemicals that determine the coloring of hair and skin. . . . The melanocytes, in turn, are responsible for chemistry that colors the hair that takes shape in the follicle and grows long enough, eventually, to be seen. . . .
>
> Melanin, the pigmentation chemical, has two components. The two basic colors predispose a hair to be dark or light or a shade between, depending on the proportion of each pigment that is genetically introduced into the hair-making process. Coloration is influenced by racial and ethnic factors, but virtually no research has been done on the existence of such influences in graying. . . .
>
> The color chemistry changes with age so that even a person who has no gray may find his or her natural hair coloring changing with advancing age. Many people experience a darkening in their coloring—directly attributable to the maturing function of the melanocytes and the varying production of melanin.
>
> With time . . . the melanocytes weaken and their pigment-producing chemistry begins to shut down. It is a gradual process and, for the period that the melanocyte is still functioning at reduced capacity, the bulb may produce a hair that is gray, or incompletely colored. In time, though, the melanocyte stops working and the hair bulb produces white hair. The process can also be influenced by a variety of diseases that prematurely—and sometimes reversibly—reduce enzyme chemistry and interfere with pigment cells. In the vast majority of cases, age and the natural evolution of melanocytes—culminating in

their cessation of function — cause graying. (Parachini, 1987, p. 2C)

However interesting that explanation may be as a description of biological process, the graying of hair is interesting primarily for sociological, not biological reasons. For of course millions of women, and increasing numbers of men, color their hair because of the negative myths and stereotypes about aging which form the basis of ageism in our society. These negative attitudes are implicit in our language: "old" is assumed to connote incompetence, misery, lethargy, unattractiveness, asexuality, and poor health, while "young" is used to imply competence, happiness, vitality, attractiveness, sexuality, and good health. People are told they're "as young" (or "only as old") as they feel, and they are admonished to "keep themselves young." When they are ill, they are said to have aged; when they recover, they're told they look younger.

The coloring of gray hair disguises the physical feature associated with aging that is most obvious and most easily changed. Such hair dyeing, in our youth-oriented culture, represents the attempt of aging people to "pass" as members of a group with greater power, privilege, and prestige than the group to which they in truth belong. In that, it is similar to the widespread use of skin lighteners by many blacks in the time preceding the Civil Rights movement.

In a patriarchal society, the power and privilege of women reside in their utility to men. They must be able and willing to bear children, and be willing to remain in a subservient position. In such a society, women beyond the menopause are useless; they obviously cannot bear children. They may also be dangerous: with the growing assertiveness that often comes to women as they age, many are unwilling to remain subservient (Guttman, 1980; Melamed, 1983; Rubin, 1981). If a woman's choices are to be either useless or dangerous as she ages, it is perhaps no wonder many women prefer to use hair color as a means of concealing — or at least underplaying — their age.

Since traditional male socialization does not encourage men to acknowledge their "weaker" feelings, women have often taken on the role of caring for men's emotional as well as their physical needs. A 54-year-old man interviewed by Barbara Gordon for her book *Jennifer Fever* says: "Men are emotionally underdeveloped, and they want women to handle the emotional side of life for them" (Gordon, 1988, p. 100). In discussing feelings of vulnerability, Jean Baker Miller argues that "women provide all sorts of personal and social supports to help keep men going and to keep them and the total society from admitting that better arrangements are needed" (Miller, 1976, p. 32).

The fact that women expend far more time, money, and effort in attempts to retain a youthful appearance than do men may well represent an aspect of such emotional caretaking. By providing men their own age (usually their husbands, but sometimes their lovers) with a false-faced mirror of youth, they may be attempting to protect such men from the emotional reality of aging and eventual death. In the film *Moonstruck*, a white-haired Olympia Dukakis asks, "Why do men chase women?" and answers herself: "Because they fear death." I once heard a man say to his gray-haired wife, without rancor: "I only feel old when I look at you."

At the same time, of course, the woman may be protecting herself, or at least attempting to do so. A gray-haired or white-haired woman is often seen as motherly, and sexual attraction to the mother is taboo. In *About Men*, Phyllis Chesler writes:

> When a wife grows "old" — *as old as his mother once was* — a man must renounce his interest in Her once again. Only the blood of strange women, the blood of ever-younger women, can be pursued without incestuous guilt. (Chesler, 1978, p. 80)

If a woman believes that maintaining a youthful appearance in itself will enable her to attract or "keep" a man, however, she may well be disappointed. In Gordon's reports on a series of interviews with older men who are in relationships with younger women, she extracts their reasons for preferring such women: adoration, which they are unlikely to receive from an age peer; "liberation backlash"; the "scarring factor" of unhappy long-term marriages to women their own age; and "innocence." A 60-year-old lawyer says:

I want someone young to love me. I want someone young and fresh and new to be attracted to me. I don't want a forty-five-year-old woman who looks great for her age, young for her age. No matter how great she looks, she's still forty-five. (Gordon, 1988, p. 100)

Fortunately, not all older men are so emotionally retarded. It will be interesting to see what kinds of attitudes today's young men, having grown up in a world where gender arrangements are changing, will have toward older women when they themselves grow old.

The assumption that women are no longer sexual beings when they have passed their childbearing years is clearly an aspect of patriarchy. The desexualizing effect of gray hair is well illustrated by the experience of a friend of mine, who had grayed in her late teens and had never colored her hair. When she was in her late thirties she dyed her hair black, on a dare. The next day, when she went to the gym she had been attending for some time, she suddenly materialized for men who had not previously noticed her.

Such magical invisibility is not only sexual; it is pervasive, similar to that noted long ago for blacks by Ralph Ellison in *Invisible Man* (1952) and James Baldwin in *Nobody Knows My Name* (1961). The title of Barbara Macdonald's powerful treatise on ageism, *Look Me in the Eye* (1983), addresses the fact that, in most social circumstances, women as well as men seldom make eye contact with the old, whom they simply do not see. If old women are not ignored, they are often subjected to a condescending head-patting kindliness which suggests that its recipient is unintelligent, uneducated, and incompetent. That women should want to avoid such treatment as far as possible is understandable, and they may be able to avoid it for a time by coloring their gray hair.

Sexism in combination with ageism also causes women problems in the job market as they age. Many women dye their hair because they fear, perhaps with good reason, that they might lose their jobs, or find it difficult to obtain jobs, if their gray hair were visible. In many professional circles, gray hair on women is considered unprofessional. Office workers in particular are often chosen for youthful physical appearance. A story frequently heard from highly competent female clerical workers in their forties and fifties is of waiting for a job interview in competition with young inexperienced women, and seeing one of those women selected for the job (Leonard, 1982).

Interestingly, however, gray hair can be an advantage for a woman who is already in a position of authority. For example, a friend of mine who was a medical resident found her students much easier to manage when she let her naturally gray hair appear. I myself suspect that my almost-white hair gives me "clout," even though I entered my profession, clinical psychology, late in life. (One might assume that having gray or white hair would be an advantage for those working with an older population, as I do; but the majority of older women I know who work with the elderly dye their hair—perhaps out of fear of being identified with their clients?)

In the personal sphere, if not in that of employment, lesbians would seem to have less incentive than their straight sisters to dye their gray hair; lesbian women are less likely to be obsessed with youth and appearance than are heterosexual women (Doress & Siegal, 1987). But prejudices against *old* women are intact among most lesbians, as indicated in Macdonald's *Look Me in the Eye* (1983) and Baba Copper's *Over the Hill: Reflections on Ageism Between Women* (1988). Copper writes:

> Lesbian youth worship differs little from heterosexual youth worship. The deprivation of sexual recognition between women which takes place after middle age (or the point when a woman no longer passes for young) includes withdrawal of the emotional work which women do to keep the flow of social interactions going: compliments, questions, teasing, touching, bantering, remembering details, checking back, supporting. (Copper, 1988, pp. 29-30)

Considering the combination of ageism with sexism, it is not surprising that far more women than men color their gray hair—45 percent of women in their forties and fifties (Doress & Siegal, 1987) and 8 percent of men (La Ferla, 1988). In a description of male and female ideals in advertising, the ideal woman's hair is "not gray," while that of the ideal man is "any color, even gray"

(Melamed, 1983, p. 121). Hollywood "stars" over the age of fifty are living testimony to the sexist aspect of ageism: almost all of the men that age are gray or white-haired (and/or balding), while almost all of the women are blondes, brunettes, or redheads. Since women begin to gray sooner than men, that is obviously not a natural gender difference. Barbara Stanwyck, now gloriously white-haired, is one of the few film actresses who has never attempted to hide her age, by either word or deed.

Most of the older female actors on television dye their hair, including the woman most often cited as a role model for older women, 63-year-old Angela Lansbury, the star of "Murder She Wrote." Of the four older women on "Golden Girls," the two characters who do not color their hair are Sophia, a rude and inconsiderate woman in her eighties (whose rudeness is presumably funny because she is old), and her daughter Dorothy (Bea Arthur), who is very tall, deep-voiced, and powerful—clearly not the essence of traditional femininity.

The belief that aging is more negative for women than for men has a long history. Lois Banner, in *American Beauty*, her study of attitudes toward American women's physical appearance, quotes a *Harper's Bazaar* article from 1892 which noted that men did not have to look young to be appreciated; they could be considered attractive at any age. For women, "on some level their physical appearance would be judged and their approximation to a youthful standard measured" (Banner, 1983, p. 225).

Despite the advances of feminism, the ageist standards of appearance were seldom challenged before the last few years—probably because the majority of women in the latest wave of the movement could, until relatively recently, have considered themselves young. Now that the Baby Boom generation is entering middle age, however, that situation is beginning to change; the Boston Women's Health Collective, for example, with the publication of the excellent guide, *Ourselves, Growing Older*, has now acknowledged that women beyond menopause have both bodies and selves (Doress & Siegal, 1987).

In general, increasing attention is being paid to the "older [i.e., middle-aged] woman," with innumerable magazine stories and newspaper articles about well-known women (such as Diahann Carroll, Joan Collins, Jane Fonda, Ali McGraw) turning forty or even fifty, proclaiming that they have no problems with growing older. The message they give about age, however, is a mixed one: "It's all right to get older as long as you look as young as possible." (Can one imagine a Civil Rights movement with the slogan "Black is beautiful as long as you look as white as possible"?) That the normal physical signs of age, particularly wrinkles and gray hair, are unattractive is usually assumed without question. The assumption that women "lose their looks" as they age is implicit in the frequent description of a woman as "good-looking for a woman her age."

The film *Moonstruck* also contains a somewhat mixed message about gray hair. When Cher, as a supposedly dowdy woman, goes to her hairdresser to become transformed, the entire salon breathes a sign of relief that they can finally get rid of her "awful gray hair." But the Nicolas Cage character fell in love with her when her hair was still gray.

Another example of this ambivalence about age is the new magazine "for the woman who wasn't born yesterday," *Lear's*. Founded by Frances Lear, the ex-wife of the television producer Norman Lear, and launched in early 1988, it is a glossy magazine for "women over 40" — wealthy women. (As such, of course, it ignores the reality that the weighted mean of pooled median incomes for women age 45 and over is $7,550 — Wang, 1988.) Though it does regularly include women's ages, and does indeed show faces with some visible wrinkles, gray hair is not in particular abundance. Frances Lear herself, as photographs indicate, is flamboyantly white-haired. But an examination of the first five issues reveals only one "cover woman" who may possibly have a few gray hairs; four have dark brown hair, and one light brown. Among the hundreds of women in the stories and advertisements, there are photographs of only thirty obviously gray-haired or white-haired women. (This total counts as one a photographic essay of a gray-haired yoga teacher — with a slim, taut, flexible body — in the second issue.) The possibility of progress is suggested by the sixth issue (January/February 1989), which includes four full-page close-up photographs of gray- and white-haired women in their sixties and seventies, with pores, wrinkles, and age lines attractively visible. (Interestingly, the second issue also contains an article about a totally dark-haired 70-year-old Mike Wallace. And three of the issues contain photo essays with full-page photographs of "good men," where wrinkles, gray and white hair, and baldness abound.)

One cannot, of course, blame editorial policy alone for the absence of women's gray hair in *Lear's*; many of the stories are about women who almost certainly color their hair. In that sense the magazine is simply reflecting a reality. Magazine articles which state that "Madison Avenue has given its OK for hair, at least, to look its age" (Salholz, 1985), and newspaper stories with titles such as "Gray definitely OK, more women believe" (Beck, 1988), appear occasionally, but the women who are cited in them as models of acceptable gray hair are most often relatively young women—the 34-year-old television news reporter Kathleen Sullivan, and the 27-year-old model Marie Seznec, for example. The oldest gray-haired woman mentioned in any of them is 45-year-old Tish Hooker, who models for Germaine Monteil.

But there is no doubt that mainline fashion magazines no longer consign gray hair to total oblivion. As long ago as 1984, in a *Harper's Bazaar* issue headlined "Forty and Fabulous: How to Look Younger Every Day," two expert hair colorists recommended "making the gray work for the woman rather than fighting it." One of them suggested coloring the rest of the hair in imaginative ways and letting "one or two gray hairs show" ("Sensational Hair," 1984, pp. 238-239). They even included, at the suggestion of the magazine, advice for the occasional woman who might not want to cover her gray hair.

Older gray-haired models are not readily accepted for everyday fashion assignments. Kaylan Pickford, the top "mature" model in the country, says there is not enough work for her to earn a living. Despite her slim figure, she says she is most in demand for ads about laxatives, aspirin, denture cream, and arthritis or osteoporosis medications (Lindeman, 1988).

Ultimately, the coloring of gray hair by women is an endorsement of both ageism and sexism. It also serves to perpetuate both those forms of discrimination. The world is full of gray- and white-haired women who are living testimony to the advantages of age for women, but the power of their testimony is greatly muted by their dyed hair. Older women entering the job market would probably find it much easier to be hired if the older women in the work force were more visible.

I am not aware of any overt attempts by feminists to raise consciousness specifically on the issue of gray hair, and I am aware of no published feminist research on the subject. Elissa Melamed, in her book on ageism and its effects, *Mirror, Mirror: The Terror of Not Being Young* (1983), talks at length about cosmetic surgery and skin treatment and their ageist implications, but dismisses hair dyeing with one sentence: "Covering gray is so simple and commonplace that there is no longer much emotional charge about it" (p. 134). (It is interesting, however, that in her fantasy about a pilot for a television series, the 50-year-old heroine's hair is gray.)

Internalized ageism, an acceptance of the status quo, is no doubt one reason little has been written about gray hair; at earlier points in time, a male-dominated world was also considered "simple and commonplace." Another reason may be a reluctance to "blame the victim." Women clearly are the victims of ageism, and older women may be struggling to do their best in a world where they are disproportionately the victims of poverty. While it might theoretically be better for them to challenge ageism, they may be fighting other battles which consume most of their energy.

When most women reach their sixties and seventies (like the women in the sixth *Lear's* issue noted above), they are likely to give up on pretense and become more willing to look like their gray-haired and white-haired selves. (The fact that suicide rates for white women peak between the ages of 45 and 54 — Melamed, 1983 — and drop steadily thereafter is perhaps significant here.) Several shampoos are marketed especially to enhance gray and white hair. The advent in the White House of a defiantly white-haired First Lady may well increase the social acceptability of "old" hair.

One might postulate that feminist women, being more aware of sexism and the patriarchy, would be less likely than nonfeminist women to color their gray hair. Again, I know of no research on the subject. It does seem to me that I see many more gray-haired women in Minneapolis and St. Paul, a Mecca for feminists, than I did in Houston, where I lived previously. As women increasingly accept the reality that they have value in themselves, beyond their youth and their serviceability to men, they will naturally be less likely to attempt to hide the normal effects of their age. Just as women have produced a less sexist world, so they can challenge ageism to produce a world in which women do not feel compelled to hide their age with hair dyes, face lifts, and other expensive stratagems.

The advantages of leaving gray hair untouched are many. It saves a considerable amount of both time and money. The natural affinity of hair and skin color is preserved. Skin tone also naturally changes with age, and women who color their hair usually have to expend considerable time and effort to make their faces match their hair. Unfortunately, the combination of old face and young hair is often discordant.

Hair may gray in interesting patterns, which are lost when the gray hair is colored. Women who allow their hair its natural changes also often find themselves able to wear colors that did not suit them in their younger-haired days. And they can preserve both their hair and their health: the use of hair dyes can contribute to hair loss, especially when combined with other harsh hair treatments (Winning the Battle, 1984), and petroleum-based dyes, usually in dark shades, cause cancer in laboratory animals and may pose a danger to users (Doress & Siegal, 1987).

The greatest advantage, however, is that a woman who allows her hair to gray naturally is accepting herself for who she is. She is also, in effect, challenging the ageism of a society that tells her she should be ashamed of her age and should make every effort to disguise it. Just as blacks took a physical feature associated with their blackness — naturally kinky hair — and flaunted it in the Afro, challenging the limited white standards of physical attractiveness, so aging women can flaunt their graying and white hair, challenging the blinkered standards of an ageist society.

In her fortieth year, talking about her hair (not about its grayness but its Blackness), Alice Walker wrote:

> Eventually, I knew precisely what hair wanted: it wanted to grow, to be itself, to attract lint, if that was its destiny, but to be left alone by anyone, including me, who did not love it as it was. . . . The ceiling at the top of my brain lifted; once again

my mind (and spirit) could get outside myself. (Walker, 1988, p. 53)

She calls her essay "Oppressed Hair Puts a Ceiling on the Brain."

REFERENCES

Baldwin, J. (1961). *Nobody knows my name: More notes on a native son*. New York: Dial Press.

Banner, L. (1983). *American beauty*. New York: Knopf.

Beck, B. (1988, February 3). Gray definitely OK, more women believe. Houston (Texas) *Chronicle*.

Chesler, P. (1978). *About men*. New York: Simon & Schuster.

Copper, B. (1988). *Over the hill: Reflections on ageism between women*. Freedom, CA: Crossing Press.

Doress, P. B., & Siegal, D. L. (1987). *Ourselves, growing older: Women aging with knowledge and power*. New York: Simon & Schuster.

Ellison, R. (1952). *Invisible man*. New York: Random House.

Gordon, B. (1988, September). Why older men chase younger women. *New woman*. From *Jennifer fever: Older men, younger women*. New York: Harper & Row.

La Ferla, R. (1988, January 17). Under cover: Going gray is going out. *New York Times Magazine*.

Leonard, F. (1982), with T. Sommers and V. Dean. *Not even for dogcatcher: Employment discrimination and older women*. Gray Paper No. 8. Washington, D.C.: Older Women's League.

Lindeman, B. (1988, February). Midlife beauty: The road to success for older models is a rough one. *Active Senior Lifestyles*. Kaylan Pickford has an autobiography, *Always a woman* (New York, Bantam), 1982.

Macdonald, B. (1983), with C. Rich. *Look me in the eye: Old women, aging and ageism*. San Francisco: Spinster's Ink.

Melamed, E. (1983). *Mirror, mirror: The terror of not being young*. New York: Simon & Schuster.

Miller, J. B. (1976). *Toward a new psychology of women*. Boston: Beacon Press.

Parachini, A. (1987, October 14). Scientists still haven't got to roots of gray hair. Minneapolis *Star-Tribune*, reprinted from the Los Angeles *Times*. All factual information about hair presented here is from this article.

Rubin, L. B. (1981). *Women of a certain age: The midlife search for self*. New York: Harper & Row.

Salholz, E. (1985, January 28). The look of a "certain age." *Newsweek*.

Sensational Hair (1984, August). *Harper's Bazaar*.

Walker, A. (1988, June). Oppressed hair puts a ceiling on the brain. *Ms.*

Wang, C. (1988). *Lear's* magazine, "For the woman who wasn't born yesterday: A critical review." *The Gerontologist, 28*, 600-601.

Winning the battle against hair loss (1984, August). *Harper's Bazaar*.

Reality?

Yesterday I took my eyes for granted
thought I would always see clearly
        the morning fog, the noonday sun
        the faces of those I love
        the words in all the books I cherish.

Today a cobweb dances before my eye
        black spots flicker over your face
        words in my books hide behind a veil.
A strange new world surrounds me.

The doctor dilates my pupil
        shines bright lights
        peers, probes, pokes;
his verdict   three learned words
        Posterior Vitreous Detachment.

He hands me a sheet of paper:
        diagram   explanation
holds out hope for gradual improvement
        no treatment   no cure.

My eye distorts what was reality.
Or is reality   a spiderweb?

                    —Ingrid Reti

Hidden Death:
The Sexual Effects of Hysterectomy

Dorin Schumacher, PhD

SUMMARY. While there have been some positive changes in American attitudes toward the sexuality and reproductive life of young women, little attention is paid to preserving aging women's sexuality. The tragic effects of this neglect appear in the case of hysterectomy, which every year deprives hundreds of thousands of women of normal sexual response.

A woman who is middle-aged in America has had, perhaps, more social change to cope with than American women who are now in other life stages — at least from the point of view of changes in women's lives and in social definitions of woman. She was born in the twenties or thirties, matured during the period of the "Feminine Mystique," and is now trying to survive in a world in which women are expected to achieve in education, careers and economic independence as well as in the traditional roles of wife and mother, even as traditional roles are subject to new stresses and strains. Among the changes she has seen are new concepts of female sexuality. Raised in a period of flirtation and repression, growing up with the peek-a-boo constraints of girdles and uplift bras in a time when

Dorin Schumacher has been speaking, writing, and publishing on women's issues since the 1960s. She earned a PhD in French Literature at the University of Pittsburgh in 1971. Now a mother and grandmother, she heads the Office of Industry Relations in the Purdue Research Foundation in West Lafayette, IN, where she lives with her husband. She has held faculty and executive positions in research administration at the University of Maine, Cornell University, Northern Illinois University, and Purdue. An associate at Argonne National Laboratory, she co-founded and serves as executive director of the Midwest Plant Biotechnology Consortium.

contraception was either illegal or considered immoral, when the word "abortion" could not be spoken in public, when illegal and often fatal abortions were carried out in the back alleys of America, when the process of childbirth was surrendered to obstetrical technology and control, when breast-feeding was considered harmful, she now faces a very different world.

From the point of view of female sexuality, ours is now, in many ways, a healthier, saner culture. A woman can choose when and if to have children, and can have more control over their birthing. She can understand and accept her own sexual responses, and if she feels they are inadequate can find help in her efforts to enhance them. It is probably safe to say that female sexual satisfaction is, at least on the cultural surface, considered as important as male sexual satisfaction. These things represent significant and positive social and psychological change.

But a remarkable thing about the changes in our sexual attitudes and behaviors is that the advances apply primarily to younger women. Attention is focussed on youthful sexuality and on reproduction, issues of a woman's fertile years. What about the ending of a woman's reproductive capabilities? What about menopause and other sexual issues — physical, social, and psychological — that concern women as their bodies age? In our culture of dyed hair, face lifts, and aerobics classes, these are generally glossed over and covered up as we deny the processes of aging.

Menopause was once described as a painful and shameful nightmare, just as were youthful manifestations of femaleness such as menstruation and childbirth. We now appear to have swung to the other extreme of denying any trauma associated with sexual aging and deterioration. We recognize the need to preserve male sexual potency, however. Much research is done; much concern expressed. But in the case of women, we focus on maintaining the appearance of youth as we try to ignore the reality of sexual and reproductive aging through both normal and abnormal processes. This has dangerous consequences for middle-aged and old women, whether rich or poor, educated or uneducated.

The exception to the collective denial of the realities of women's aging is the attention paid to mastectomy and the loss of a breast. There is considerable publicity about breast cancer, its early detection and treatment. There are counseling groups for women who have undergone mastectomies. Prosthesis and surgical reconstruction are available, along with information about the disease, its treatment and merits of alternative treatments. One reason for this special attention, of course, is our cancerphobia. Another is that a woman's breast has to do with the *appearance* of sexuality, especially in men's eyes. Since Americans are cancerphobes and mammaphiles, it is easy to understand our interest in the problems of breast cancer and the effects of mastectomy. However, this interest does not represent a deep understanding of female sexual experience or an awareness of the real issues around women's aging. In almost every other case, aging women are not being adequately equipped to understand, manage, and control their lives, or to protect themselves and their sexuality as they age.

A clear manifestation of this cultural failure is found in the common American medical treatment of choice for many problems associated with the physical deterioration of the female sexual/reproductive organs: hysterectomy and oophorectomy, the surgical removal of the uterus and ovaries. This is a sociopolitical, not medical, phenomenon which reflects our cultural denials and reveals the tragic consequences of such denials for middle-aged and old women. Women are led to believe that the surgery is performed in a medical context; that is why they consent to it. But theirs is not an informed consent. This radical and destructive surgery results not only in sudden menopausal changes but in some of the most extreme changes that can be brought about by sexual aging, occurring in a matter of days and weeks rather than gradually over a period of many years. It is a further reflection of our society's ignorance about and denial of female sexual aging that the facts about the irreversible sexual losses from this surgery are suppressed, ignored, and denied, often by the victims themselves. There is a terrible hidden pain and loss associated with this treatment of choice which need to be brought out in the open, acknowledged, understood, and prevented.

American women's ignorance of the physiology of their sexual/reproductive systems and the effects of aging upon them, as well as the cultural hiding of women's sexual functioning behind their reproductive systems, contribute to placing women under the control and domination of the medical profession. Most medical professionals appear similarly ignorant of the physiology and psychology of female sexual and reproductive systems. This tragic shared ignorance is in large part the result of insufficient biomedical research, which stems from inadequate research funding, which stems from our cultural denials — denials which are based on the denigration of women, fear of aging, and fears of female sexuality.

Listen to the voices of some of the women who have undergone this surgical "treatment."[1]

After my first husband and I split up, it seemed as though the world was filled with happy, close, loving families. I would drive through the park on a Sunday afternoon, past the family groups playing and picnicking together, and feel painfully aware of my aloneness and being different from the others. Eventually, I did re-establish a family group of my own, and I stopped noticing and thinking about all the other families.

A similar thing happened to me after my hysterectomy. The surgery totally destroyed my sexual response, and in my grief, I became acutely aware of the images and expressions of sexuality all around me. I suddenly began to see, for the first time as an outsider, intense sexual attraction between loving couples. Television and magazines suddenly seemed full of nubile young women shamelessly exhibiting their bodies: even pre-pubescent little girls represented the promise of future sexual flowering, as I imagined their immature uteruses inside their abdomens. All these signs of sexual love, of fertility, or of sexual potential caused me unbearable pain. I couldn't bear to walk past the sanitary napkins on drugstore and supermarket shelves. But, unlike my family situation, where I could form a new family, I could not "re-establish" my lost sexuality. It had been cut out by the surgeon's knife.

When my husband and I would try to make love like we had before my surgery, I would try calling on my old sexual fantasies to help me recover an arousal I no longer felt. But the only fantasy I could muster was the image of my mutilated abdomen, the surgeon's slashing and cutting, and my bloody uterus and ovaries being pulled out of me as I lay on the operating table.

It is hard for someone who has not experienced it to imagine sudden and complete loss of sexual desire and loss of the capacity to respond sexually. It is a terrible emotional as well as physical loss. Making love to the person you love, having an orgasm in the context of a deep emotional bond and commitment, is an experience of the coming together of one's own total sensual self and emotional self, in union with the one you love. This is not something that happens every time a couple makes love. But it happens sometimes, often only after many years of building a relationship; and when it happens it is transcendent. Losing the capacity for that experience is devastating, as you realize that you will never again be one with the person you love in the ecstasy of orgasm.

> It was the strangest thing, after my hysterectomy . . . When my sexual response to my husband was gone, I no longer felt an emotional response to him. It was as though my feeling of love for him had been connected with my whole body and its desire for him. I can't really explain it, because I know I had loved him emotionally as well as physically, but I just felt dead toward him. I no longer felt the tingling of arousal in my whole body when I went near him. I miss so much the excitement I used to feel in my body.
>
> After my surgery, when the doctor said it was ok to have sex again, my husband caressed my clitoris like he used to. He might as well have been rubbing my elbow. I had no sexual response to his touch.

The loss of one's sexuality is also social, going beyond the couple's relationship. Sexual messages in our culture assume either "normal" or superhuman sexual responses, and sexuality is a culturally important means for Americans to relate to one another. Lost sexuality disrupts our sense of ourselves as sexual beings, made up of a lifetime of sexual experiences. In women, this includes our experiences of puberty, of lovemaking, of childbearing. Suddenly all that is shaken.

What am I, if I don't have a uterus and I don't have ovaries, and I don't feel any arousal toward my husband or anyone else. Am I a woman? I still look like a woman to those around me, but I don't feel like a woman any more. What am I?

More than 670,000 hysterectomies were performed in the U.S. in 1985 (Hufnagel, 1988). Castration, or removal of the ovaries, called oophorectomy, was performed in about a third of the hysterectomies. Even where the ovaries were preserved, 30 to 50 percent of the hysterectomized women suffered ovarian failure (Hufnagel, 1988). Hysterectomy is one of the most frequently performed major surgical procedures in this country, a ranking that is particularly disturbing in view of the fact that it can only be done to half the population. Another way of looking at the numbers which reveals even more strikingly that this is a routine medical practice is the fact that only 63 percent of American women reach 65 with their uteruses intact. The truly appalling number is the estimate that only 10.5 percent of all hysterectomies performed in the U.S. between 1970 and 1984 were necessary and medically indicated (Hufnagel, 1988). Castrating women and amputating their uteruses and cervixes is being used by modern gynecologists as a "cure" for a variety of ailments, from premenstrual syndrome and abdominal pain to benign fibroid tumors, and as a prevention of cancer where no symptoms of cancer are present.

Jokes are made about eunuchs, or castrated males. The word calls to mind men who were castrated so they could be trusted to serve as guards in harems — their sexual desire and ability to have erections, orgasms, and ejaculations having been removed surgically. But no jokes are made about America's millions of castrated females. Almost no one talks about them and their sexual losses. Almost no one acknowledges their existence or their suffering. Almost no one comforts them.

The fact is that the sexual losses from the amputation of a woman's uterus and cervix and her castration by removal of her ovaries are real.[2] And they are devastating. They break up marriages. They make women suicidal (Richards, 1974; Stokes, 1986).

But there is another loss that is perhaps the most unbearable of all: the loss of being believed. The people around the woman whose

sex organs have been surgically taken out of her body, the woman
who has been castrated, do not believe that she has lost her sexual
functioning. Her doctor doesn't believe her. Her lover doesn't believe her. She doesn't read about it anywhere. There are not support
groups for her to turn to. Her experience is not validated by those
around her or by the culture in which she lives. This is the kind of
denial that can literally drive a person crazy.

> When I told my gynecologist after my surgery that I no longer
> had any sexual response, he said, 'Sex is all psychological.'
> He dismissed me, my condition, and any responsibility for my
> condition, all at the same time.

It is for her a hidden death. She cannot mourn it in public; she has
no one to turn to in private. She questions the reality of her own
experience of her body.

The facts about female sexuality are simple: the uterus, cervix,
vagina, and clitoris are the physical organs in which a woman's
primary physical/sexual sensations and orgasm are felt, the places
where they occur (Hite, 1976; Kinsey, 1953; Masters & Johnson,
1966). The ovaries, both before *and for many years after menopause,* secrete, in addition to estrogen, the hormone testosterone[3]
which triggers both sexual desire and orgasm (Sherwin & Gelfand,
1987; Sherwin, Gelfand & Brender, 1985; Zussman, Zussman,
Sunley & Bjornson, 1981). Without ovarian testosterone, without
cervix or uterus, a woman lacks the major tissues and hormone
levels needed for sexual desire and a strong and complete orgasm,
or perhaps for any orgasm at all.

> Before I had my hysterectomy, I was in sexual terms a "10."
> Now I would rate myself about a "2." I can have an orgasm
> of slight clitoral contractions, but never again will I have the
> wonderful deep uterine and vaginal contractions at orgasm that
> I had before my surgery.

* * *

> My husband and I used to have what we called our 'nooners.'
> We would come home for lunch and make love — the ecstasy I

felt from his erect penis thrusting against my cervix was incredible. Now I feel nothing at all.

It is thus difficult to understand how a physician can believe that sex is "all in a woman's head," that a woman's sexual dysfunction after hysterectomy is purely psychological. And yet this is today's mythology which allows women to give up their sexuality to the surgeon's knife.

The facts about female sexuality appear simple. Harder to understand is the denial of the evidence of women's subjective accounts of their experience, and now the evidence of scientific investigation. The question is not only how this callous butchery and sexual abuse of women by the medical profession has happened, but why it continued to happen. Why do women continue to allow their doctors to remove their sex organs? Why has there not been a great public outcry against this barbaric and outdated practice?

I can't believe I let this surgery be done to me. I am an educated woman, a microbiologist who was working in a university research laboratory. How could I not have known?

* * *

When I told my male colleagues I had to take time off to have a hysterectomy, many of them looked sad. In retrospect, they must have known more than the women did. I guess it is what they lost with their wives. But nobody told me what I would lose.

The doctor called it "removing my ovaries." It wasn't until after the surgery and I felt my sexual numbness that I realized that the correct word is "castration." I had let myself be castrated, and I hadn't even known until it was too late that's what was going to be done to me.

Since I have claimed that the ongoing epidemic of surgeons hysterectomizing women is a sociopolitical phenomenon, I will speculate as to what the contributing sociopolitical factors are.

1. Most American medicine is based on a disease model rather than a wellness model and is oriented toward aggressive acute care, rather than toward prevention or toward long term, individualized

care. The rewards and reinforcements lie with the practice of acute care. Acute care, such as the surgical procedure hysterectomy, with its accompanying hospitalization and payments to the physicians (surgeons, radiologists, anesthesiologists, pathologists), provides more income to hospitals and physicians than does the prevention of uterine and ovarian disorders or their long term treatment. With an operation that is the second most common surgery in the U.S. and the leading major surgery, we are talking about big business for doctors and hospitals, estimated at $1.7 billion dollars in 1985 for the surgical procedure alone (Stokes, 1986).

There are some caring researchers and practitioners who have developed and tested both medical and surgical treatment alternatives to hysterectomy involving such things as the administration of hormones and less radical, more reconstructive surgeries. Information about these approaches is not widely disseminated either within the medical community or to the public. A handful of people are working on developing treatments, but they are swimming upstream against a very powerful current. Dr. Vicki Hufnagel (1988) describes "Female Reconstructive Surgery," a surgical approach that she and her team have developed which is corrective, as opposed to amputational. Instead of taking out the uterus, new technologies such as the laser are being used to remove pre-cancerous cells from its lining (Loffer's study cited in Poirot, 1986). Investigators in Scandinavia have discovered that surgical removal of the uterus and preservation of the cervix, instead of the removal of both uterus and cervix, prevents sexual dysfunction (Kilkku, Gronroos, Hirvonen & Rauramo, 1983).

2. We have a naive faith in the healing powers of modern medicine and the authority of the physician. If there is a procedure that is commonplace, such as hysterectomy, there is a tendency to believe that it must be effective and appropriate. The frightening alternative may be to believe in the ignorance, superstition, sexism, and even misogyny of the medical profession — at least as far as women's sex organs are concerned.

3. In addition to the fact that the American physician is notoriously authoritarian by selection and by training, the old male-female stereotypes continue to operate in the male doctor-female patient relationship. Women too often see their physicians as strong,

wise, caring professionals who have their patients' best interests at heart, and see themselves as weak, helpless, medically ignorant, and dependent on their male physicians. So after a lifetime pattern of not questioning their doctors' knowledge, skill, judgment, or motivation, they are ready to believe they need a hysterectomy, and are even ready to believe that their sexual dysfunction post-hysterectomy has some other cause.

4. Biomedical research is still carried out primarily by men, and the decisions about which research proposals get funded are still made primarily by men. Studying female sexuality and the changes that take place in a woman's sexual/reproductive system as she ages, and developing non-invasive clinical approaches to ameliorate the negative changes, do not attract the big research funding that helps build long lists of publications. They are not as "sexy" or perceived to be as "important" as research on AIDS, cancer, or heart disease (Sukenik, 1984).

5. Our culture looks upon a woman's sexual organs as reproductive organs. Children's "sex education" is typically "reproduction education," with the emphasis placed on the ovaries, the uterus, and the vagina as baby-making places, rather than as the loci of a woman's sexual response and pleasure. Thus it is all too easy for a woman and her doctor to agree to "take it all out" around the age of menopause, when her child-bearing years are over. Doctors and their patients are ready to believe that these have become "useless" organs, sources of potential disease and decay. Physicians actually believe that hysterectomies are good for women having problems with their sexual/reproductive organs (Doress & Siegal, 1987). If ever proof was needed that doctors don't listen to their patients, this is it!

6. Young girls and women are not taught to treasure their sexuality, nor are they taught the basic physiological facts about their sexuality. The ignorance we permit makes it possible for them later to give up their sex organs, in the mistaken belief they are "protecting their health." Tragically, by the time they reach an understanding, it is too late.

7. Young women are not taught that the uterus and the ovaries are an important part of their health and well-being and of their bodies' functioning, even beyond the sexual and reproductive functions.

Not only important for the sensations of orgasm, the uterus is part of the endocrine system, with important endocrine and immune functions, producing proteins, hormones, and the anti-inflammatory prostaglandins. The uterus is also important as a support structure for proper pelvic anatomy. And it is now believed that many of the long-term complications found in post-hysterectomized and castrated women, including osteoporosis, arthritis, cardiovascular problems, and emotional problems, result from the loss of the ovaries. There is evidence that women who have had a hysterectomy are at increased risk for heart disease (Punnonen, Ikalainen & Seppala, 1987). Adequate testosterone, much of it secreted by the ovaries, interacting with brain chemistry, is not only essential for a positive sex drive, but also for energy, vitality and feelings of well-being (Hufnagel, 1988; Sherwin & Gelfand, 1985).

8. The male model, and thus the medical model, of female sexuality appears to be based primarily on what a man can see, feel, use, and enjoy: the vagina and the breasts, neither of which typically is the source of a woman's greatest orgasmic response. Thus male physicians could believe that a hysterectomy does not affect a woman's sexuality. After all, while her vagina may be a little shorter after the hysterectomy has removed both her uterus and her cervix, it still can accommodate an erect penis. So how could she not still feel the same pleasure?

9. Gynecologists will often promise women that estrogen replacement therapy will restore everything to "normal" after the hysterectomy. But estrogen has no effect on sexual response (Sherwin & Gelfand, 1987; Sherwin, Gelfand & Brender, 1985). It may keep vaginal tissue supple, so the vagina can still accommodate the erect penis, but it does not enable the vagina to feel aroused.

> The doctor told me that the hysterectomy would be "less trouble" and "easier" than having hormone therapy—that I would tolerate the surgery well since I hadn't had previous abdominal surgery and had no scar tissue. She made it sound like a simple, safe procedure. She said they do hormone replacement therapy with estrogen, and the estrogen, which I could take the rest of my life, would maintain the tissues in

their normal state. She didn't tell me that the tissues that were left — my vagina and my clitoris — while the estrogen might keep them supple and lubricated, would feel numb. And so it wouldn't much matter how "normal" they might look, or how supple and lubricated the tissues would be.

10. Most physicians and biomedical researchers are men. From the late teens onward, male libido and potency decline. A woman's libido and response peak later and last longer, normally well past menopause, increased and enhanced by additional blood vessels formed during pregnancy. The older male gynecologist is likely to have declining sexual interest and response; it would be easy for him to assume, and even want to believe, that it is the same for a woman. He may assume there is no great loss if she doesn't have strong orgasms any more, because he doesn't either. It could be hard for him to want to protect the strong sexual response a woman has in her forties, fifties, sixties and beyond. Perhaps the surgeon wishes to deny his own loss of potency, and does not want to believe that women are superior in this aspect of their physiology and pleasure.

My doctor told me that after menopause, the ovaries cease functioning and become "useless" organs. He said I might as well have them out so I would be safe from ovarian cancer. He said I would be going through menopause anyway in a couple of years.

11. There is a tendency, in modern American medical practice, to take a psychological approach to the treatment of women's complaints. Thus the overprescription of tranquilizers for women. If women's other physical symptoms are treated as psychological symptoms by physicians, then certainly a decline in their sexual functioning post-hysterectomy will be too.

12. Women in our culture typically do not discuss with each other the quality or frequency of their orgasms; so when after being hysterectomized they no longer can have orgasms, they can't talk about that either. The taboos are strong; the shared language to express their losses is not there. The horror stories are not being

freely shared among women so they can learn from each other's experiences.

Surprisingly, it seems as though some husbands can talk about the sexual effects of hysterectomy more easily than their wives can:

> My wife can't have hormone replacement therapy because she is diabetic, so she still has hot flashes. She doesn't say anything, but I know she is suffering; I can see it in her face. We don't touch any more, since her surgery. I still love her, but I miss making love to her. We don't talk about it. My mother, who had a hysterectomy years ago, asked me once if my wife was "different" since her operation. I guess it really affects women that way.

* * *

> My wife had a hysterectomy years ago. We didn't want any more children, and we are Catholic, so they did the operation. She doesn't respond sexually to me. But she knows if she doesn't submit to me, I will leave her.

13. To have a strong sex drive and an active sex life is almost synonymous with success in America. Our culture is full of images designed to stimulate and promote sexual feelings and their expression. So what woman is going to stand up in public and admit to the loss of her sexuality? There are terrible feelings of failure and shame associated with the awareness that one has been castrated and no longer is sexually functional, especially if one participated, however unwittingly, in allowing oneself to be castrated.

14. The obstetrician is the loving doctor who delivers the beautiful baby. The gynecologist is the misguided or mercenary surgeon who removes an aging woman's sex organs (or else is the doctor who, not wanting to face the increased risk of obstetrical malpractice suits, finds doing hysterectomies "safer"). A woman is not prepared for the switch, not realizing she may be faced with a Dr. Jekyll and a Dr. Hyde situation. She trusts the obstetrician/gynecologist. And if her doctor is a woman, she may be even more trusting, but be in exactly the same danger. Women doctors are trained the

same as men doctors, and in order to be "successful," need to become part of the male medical establishment.

15. The potential for abuse is so great that there has been some publicity about unnecessary hysterectomies, but it is generally thought that all that is needed to prevent abuse is for a woman to get "a second opinion." This second opinion is usually obtained from another doctor trained in the same medical "routine," sharing the same belief system, a participant in the same sociopolitical system.

16. As I discussed earlier, there has been tremendous publicity given to the negative effects of mastectomy on women and much support given to women who have to undergo the surgery. Everyone knows that a woman feels terrible about losing a breast, and she doubts she is still desirable. Nelson Rockefeller brought mastectomy out of the closet and talked publicly about his wife's two mastectomies and Betty Ford talked publicly about hers; but what man in public life has gone to the press and discussed his wife's hysterectomy? What woman in public life has discussed her own castration? Where are the support groups for women who have had a hysterectomy?[4] Where are the education programs for the early prevention and detection of uterine deterioration? Where is the publicity and discussion and information about treatment alternatives to hysterectomy and oophorectomy? Where is the public discussion about the permanent adverse, devastating consequences of the removal of the ovaries, about the statistically low risks of ovarian cancer versus the high probability of adverse effects from the destruction of an important part of a woman's endocrine system, about the importance of the ovarian hormones, about the fact that the ovaries continue to secrete important sex hormones for many years after menopause, and about the many important functions of the uterus?[5]

Since most hysterectomies are elective and are done for benign conditions, the complications and adverse effects of hysterectomies represent a case of "iatrogenic" or doctor-induced disease. An all-out attack on the practice of hysterectomies is thus an attack on the medical profession. The popular press is not in the business of carrying articles that attack its heavy advertisers. So what they do not avoid because of squeamishness or prudery on the one hand, or sexism on the other, they avoid because of fears of criticizing a large and powerful segment of American society.

Now there is evidence that publicity in the mass media can be effective in reducing the frequency with which hysterectomies are performed. The rate of hysterectomies in an area of Switzerland fell twenty-five percent after a public information campaign about the procedure was carried in the local press ("Surgery Drop May," 1989).

17. It is enlightening to compare the cultural treatment of the sexual effects of hysterectomy-oophorectomy with the treatment of male sexual disorders. One can find lengthy, concerned, thorough discussions in the popular press about the possible adverse sexual effects of prostate surgery, for example, and descriptions of various new (and expensive) medical technologies and treatments for loss of potency ("New Treatments," 1988; Reinisch, 1987). The sexual effects of hysterectomy-oophorectomy are either denied or they are glossed over (Conrad, 1988; Reinisch, 1988).

18. Our legal system reflects the same biases, prejudices, myths, and misinformation we see manifested in other parts of our culture. Unlike other sociopolitical problems, sexual damage from hysterectomy is not a problem that can be solved by litigation. Lawyers and the courts do not believe that a woman's loss of twenty, thirty, forty or more years of sexual pleasure is a compensable loss (Stokes, 1986).

If the problem of hysterectomy is located in the sociopolitical issues discussed above, we must seek a sociopolitical solution. By that I mean a re-education of men and women to value a woman's sexual/reproductive organs, not for the products they can sell, but for what they contribute to a woman's happiness, health, and sense of vitality and well-being. Loving the uterus means loving all the signs of a woman's fertility: the bleeding, the cramps, the smells, and secretions, even loving premenstrual syndrome! It means selecting lovers and physicians who also treasure all those things and want to protect and preserve them.

Loving a woman's sexuality for what it gives *her* means enabling her to love her first signs of sexual arousal and the sexual desire and responses she feels throughout her life. It means encouraging her to express, articulate, defend and protect her sexual responses and be proud of them. It means giving up the megabucks American industry makes by selling superficial adolescence to women: plastic sur-

gery on breasts, wrinkle creams, hair dyes. It means giving up the
hygienic approach to female sexuality in the Twiggy-like hips, the
perfumed douches. It means giving up the ambitious career-related
illusion that women can be the same as men, and that they have the
same needs and concerns as men. It means loving our bodies
young, middle-aged, and old. It means becoming sensitive to, be-
lieving, and following the inner messages of our bodies and refus-
ing to package them for external consumption. Dr. Vicki Hufnagel
(1988) writes of

> the truly awe-inspiring complexity of the entire female repro-
> ductive system. . . . tied to nearly every aspect of a woman's
> health, including her blood chemistry, brain chemistry, neuro-
> logical system, endocrine system, skeletal system, immune
> system, body fat, sexuality, and psychological functioning
> . . . the natural beauty and power of our biological uniqueness,
> which I believe makes us stronger—not "weaker." (pp. 243-
> 244)

If we can love ourselves and love the integrity of our bodies, we
will be able to recognize the castration of American women for
what it is—female patient abuse. We have brought wife-beating and
date rape out of the closet. It is time the sexual abuse of women by
the medical profession is brought out of the closet, given its proper
name, prosecuted, and prevented.

It's a tall order. But it seems to me that if women have been able
to take back control of childbirth in some measure, they can also
take back and keep control of their uteruses and ovaries as sources
of *their own* sexual pleasure.

> It has been five years since I had a "complete" hysterectomy,
> including the removal of my ovaries. After the surgery I no
> longer felt any sexual desire or arousal. I finally found a doc-
> tor who believed me and said it was the effect of the surgery.
> He also told me, after examining my pre-surgery pathology
> report, that my uterus had been normal for my age. He pre-
> scribed both estrogen and testosterone for me, which I take
> regularly. The testosterone has restored some sexual function-
> ing, but it is a pale shadow of what I used to feel. The psycho-
> logical pain that I feel from the loss of my sexual functioning,

the loss of the beautiful love-making my husband and I shared, the knowledge that I will never have this again in my life, is still so unbearable I can't talk about it without crying. I have been in psychotherapy ever since the surgery, and I still find the pain of my sexual losses unbearable. I am now in my early fifties and that part of my life is ended forever. I don't think I will ever get over it.

NOTES

1. The voices in this article represent a composite of the hysterectomized and castrated women and their husbands and lovers I have talked with.
2. Stokes (1986, p. 59) refers to the findings of Newton's study of "reduced sexual drive in 60 percent of women who had had their uterus and both ovaries removed. Forty percent of the women who'd had hysterectomies never resumed sexual intercourse." She says other researchers report that between 20 and 42 percent of women studied abstain from sexual intercourse following hysterectomy. Utian (1975, p. 100) finds a "high incidence of decreased or absent libido in all groups of patients having undergone the operation of hysterectomy, irrespective of whether the ovaries had been conserved or not." Zussman, Zussman, Sunley and Bjornson (1981, p. 725) refer to studies' findings that "33% to 46% of women report decreased sexual response after hysterectomy-oophorectomy," and report that, "a substantial percentage of women report decreased satisfaction with or without oophorectomy" (p. 728).
3. The adrenal gland also is a source of testosterone, so oophorectomy may result in a decrease of sexual desire and response rather than a total loss. Studies have shown that the combination of oophorectomy and adrenalectomy results in sudden and total loss of libido (Sherwin, Gelfand & Bender, 1985). Many women report experiencing a total loss of sexual desire and response from oophorectomy alone.
4. One organization trying to make a difference is the HERS Foundation (Hysterectomy Educational Resources and Referral Services), Bala Cynwyd, Pennsylvania.
5. Notable exceptions are books written recently such as the ones by Stokes (1966), Hufnagel (1988), and Doress, Siegel et al. (1987).

REFERENCES

Conrad, P. (1988, May). What you'd like to know from your gynecologist but are too embarrassed to ask. *Good Housekeeping*, 135-136.
Doress, P. B., Siegal, D. L. and The Midlife and Older Women Book Project in cooperation with The Boston Women's Health Book Collective. (1987). *Ourselves, growing older*. New York: Simon & Schuster.

Hite, S. (1976). *The Hite report*. New York: Macmillan.

Hufnagel, V. (1988). *No more hysterectomies*. New York: New American Library.

Kilkku, P., Gronroos, M., Hirvonen, T., & Rauramo, L. (1983). Supravaginal uterine amputation vs. hysterectomy: Effects on libido and orgasm. *Acta Obstetrica Gynecologica Scandinavica, 62* (2), 147-152.

Kinsey, A. (1953). *Sexual Behavior in the Human Female*. Philadelphia: W. B. Saunders.

Masters, W. H., Johnson, V. (1966). *Human Sexual Response*. Boston: Little, Brown.

Poirot, C. (1986, December). Laser surgery latest alternative to those seeking a hysterectomy. *The Indianapolis Star*.

Punnonen, R., Ikalainen, M., and Seppala, E. (1987). Premenopausal hysterectomy and risk of cardiovascular diseases. *Lancet, 1*, 1139.

Reinisch, J. (1987, December). The Kinsey Report. *The Indianapolis Star*.

Reinisch, J. (1988, March). The Kinsey Report. *The Indianapolis Star*.

Richards, D. H. (1974). A post-hysterectomy syndrome. *Lancet 1* 983-985.

Sherwin, B. B., and Gelfand, M. M. (1985). Differential Symptom response to parenteral estrogen and/or androgen administration in the surgical menopause. *American Journal of Obstetrics and Gynecology, 151* (2), 153-160.

Sherwin, B. B., and Gelfand, M. M. (1987). The role of androgen in the maintenance of sexual functioning in oophorectomized women. *Psychosomatic Medicine, 49*, 397-409.

Sherwin, B. B., Gelfand, M. M., and Brender, W. (1985). Androgen enhances sexual motivation in females: A prospective crossover study of sex steroid administration in the surgical menopause. *Psychosomatic Medicine, 47*, 339-351.

Staff. (1988, April). New treatments for prostate enlargement and prostate cancer preserve potency. *Sex Over Forty*, p. 5.

Stokes, N. M. (1986). *The castrated woman: What your doctor won't tell you about hysterectomy*. New York: Franklin Watts.

Sukenik, J. W. (1984). *Sex after hysterectomy*. Paper presented at Second Annual Hysterectomy Conference, The HERS Foundation, Philadelphia, PA.

Surgery drop may be tied to publicity, report says. (1989, January 4). *The Wall Street Journal*, p. B4.

Utian, W. H. (1975). Effect of hysterectomy, oophorectomy and estrogen therapy on libido. *International Journal of Gynaecology and Obstetrics, 13*, 97-100.

Zussman, L., Zussman, S., Sunley, R., and Bjornson, E. (1981). Sexual response after hysterectomy-oophorectomy: Recent studies and reconsideration of psychogenesis. *American Journal of Obstetrics and Gynecology, 140*, 725-729.

Sonnet

When nearly every other sonnet speaks
Of love so there it is: the empty page,
The silent phone, the rattling night, the weeks,
The days, the hours that all add up to rage—
The rage to run and not to wait and pine
Like all the good Victorian ladies wait;
Like good girls did in nineteen-forty-nine
Their pleated skirts concealed their loving hate.
Now Older Women learn to "share" and trust
The men they choose are either straight or gay;
The flirts and lockets surely turned to rust—
New games are starting: some will go (some stay).
O daughters, sons and other children heed:
Just grab your loves from time's confusing speed.

—Mira Josefowitz Spektor
262 Central Park West
New York, NY 10024

Love and Work After 60:
An Integration of Personal
and Professional Growth
Within a Long-Term Marriage

Rachel Josefowitz Siegel, MSW

SUMMARY. An exploration of growth and change involving external crisis and internal shifts of awareness during a therapist's transition from midlife to old age. Focus is on the continuing need to balance and renegotiate work and family within a framework of creativity, professional opportunities, aging, spouse's illness, and changing social climate.

While the decade of the sixties is a major transitional period for both women and men, my comments focus primarily on my own experience as it illustrates some of the transitional processes that married women may undergo at this period in the life span. Specifi-

---

Rachel Josefowitz Siegel earned her MSW from Syracuse University in 1973, at the age of 49. She is a psychotherapist in private practice in Ithaca, NY. She is a founding member of the Feminist Therapy Institute and has served two terms on its Steering Committee. She was a member of the first editorial board of *Women & Therapy*. With Joan Hamerman Robbins, she co-edited *Women Changing Therapy, New Assessments, Values and Strategies in Feminist Therapy*, and has written and lectured on feminist therapy and a variety of women's mental health issues. Her current focus is on celebrating the diversity of women's lives, women over sixty, the idealization and blaming of mothers, and issues affecting Jewish women, including the Jewish American Princess stereotyping and harassment.

This article has grown out of a paper presented at the International Conference for the Advancement of Private Practice of Clinical Social Work, Cape Cod, MA, August 1988.

Reprints can be obtained from Rachel Josefowitz Siegel, MSW, 108 W Buffalo St., Ithaca, NY 14850.

cally, I explore the interaction of personal and professional growth and development that can occur in the life of a woman therapist after midlife. The extent to which my remarks can be generalized to other women of my generation is of course limited by the particular circumstances of my life and the predominantly white, middle-class, well-educated, and heterosexual ambience of my social environment. My perceptions were often confirmed and greatly enriched in talking with other women my age about our own aging and in reading the current writings by and about old women [Adelman (Ed.), 1986; Alexander, Berrow, Domitrovich, Donnely, McLean (Eds.), 1986; Copper, 1988; Doress, Siegal & The Midlife and Older Women Book Project with The Boston Women's Health Book Collective (Eds.) 1987; Macdonald & Rich, 1983; Walker, 1985]. Conversations took place with friends, colleagues, and clients, at workshops and gatherings of old women, and especially in my support group for women over sixty.

I am sixty-four years old. Like many women of my generation, I am now at the height of my professional career, having started it in my late forties. My private psychotherapy practice is flourishing; I have a sense of competence in my clinical work that is stronger and more secure than it was a few years ago; I have published, and I get frequent requests to present papers and do workshops.

On the other hand, I have less energy than I did five years ago. My blood pressure fluctuates erratically under stress or fatigue. I need more time to recover from travel or from other variations in routine, and I have less tolerance for early rising or late nights. I have more need and inclination for leisure and quiet times. At times my memory feels overloaded. I find it difficult to fit in as much writing or public speaking as I would like or to see as many clients, lead as many workshops or groups as I can imagine doing. I wish I had more time and energy to see my friends and family, to visit with my grandchildren, to travel just for fun and to catch up with some of the fascinating reading in my books and journals.

I don't know how much of my slowing down is due to my own aging, and how much of it is due to the stress of adjusting to my seventy-two year old husband's retirement and the deterioration of his health during these past five years. There is no doubt that my partner's heart attack and his subsequent coronary by-pass surgery have been significant turning points for each of us as individuals and for the nature and quality of our relationship. We are both feeling the effects of age and are affected by each other's physical, emotional and professional well-being.

Most of our friends and relatives are making life changes triggered by forced retirement or age-related health problems. Some have retired or slowed down to semi-retirement; they spend part of the winter in warmer climates if they can afford to do so. They travel more, spend more time being sociable and visiting extended family. I feel again the external and internal pressure to return to the familiar roles of full-time wife, home-maker and care-giver. A new role has emerged with its own attractions and responsibilities; I call it the geriatric jet set traveler, responding to the needs or celebrations of close friends and relatives.

The medical crises of late life and the death of significant age-mates have created a renewed bonding and sharing with our siblings and with those old friends who are still alive, throwing me back into a world of unexamined and male-centered heterosexuality. Here my feminist activities and our egalitarian life style are viewed with a mixture of amusement and discomfort. In contrast, I am often the oldest woman present and the only one still married among my feminist friends. The effort to live in both these worlds seems to reflect the changing mores and values of our time. My life feels richer, more complex, and at times more difficult for choosing to maintain strong ties within both camps. Again I feel the never-ending inner conflict between new friends and old friends, between the importance of my professional work and the automatic assumption that my family and familial relationships should be primary.

The pressure to choose between family and profession has entered a new phase. At my age there are no role models for integrating these two vital aspects of life. The stress feels more acute and more constant than it did ten years ago, when death was not a steady companion, when my partner's life seemed less precarious, when we were both fully engaged in our professional lives and when feminist consciousness was on the rise rather than suffering from backlash. Within my marriage, the tension of trying to combine the pleasures and responsibilities of work and family gets intertwined with an inner tension between my wish for greater intimacy on the one hand and sufficient distance on the other.

We are experiencing a shifting of roles in yet another way. My professional commitments now take me away from home more frequently while my husband Ben has almost eliminated his professional trips. He now spends more time at home and has to cope with creating his own daily structure. Because of his precarious health, we both feel an undercurrent of anxiety, especially when I am out of town. Our fears are difficult to talk about and can easily turn into irritability. Tensions intensify between us when I leave or return from professional conferences or when Ben anticipates or recovers from yet one more medical episode. When these two conditions overlap we find it difficult to cope with our combined anxieties. Imagine, for instance, trying to make unrefundable plane reservations for a conference next month, when neither of us knows how well he will have recovered by then from this week's unexpected surgery. At times, these combined pressures get played out in conflict between us, or in a daily round of compromises, decisions and resolutions made in a bittersweet atmosphere of loving concern, mixed with frustration and impatience.

Sexuality continues to be an important aspect of our lives together, but there have been periods when illness or the side effects of medication have made sexual activity problematic, causing added frustrations in an overstressed environment. In our generation, it is not easy to find experts or friends who are both knowledgeable and comfortable enough to talk explicitly about sex. We are confronted with ageist attitudes about sex, and have run into medical practitioners who trivialize or ridicule our questions about sexual functioning. The emotional and physical accommodations to the sexual changes of our aging bodies have been challenging and complex. We have felt isolated and angry about the lack of understanding or support in this aspect of our well-being. Most research and literature about sexuality ends with a paragraph on midlife. Books like *Sex After 60* (Butler & Lewis, 1976) or *Love, Sex, and Aging* (Brecher, 1984) have helped us feel less isolated.

On a positive note, we have developed a maturity and flexibility that usually allows us to respond appropriately and differentially to each situation, even finding new solutions to old dilemmas; on a

negative note, many situations call forth a somewhat painful or con-
flictual renegotiation of the interactional contract between us. It
comes as somewhat of a surprise to find that our relationship is in
transition at this late stage of life. My image of being married in old
age had been of a couple who have long ago completed their adjustments to each other's ways, and are by now comfortably set in well
established patterns. In talking with other women my age, I found
that the decade of the sixties is indeed one of major and minor
changes in significant aspects of life, including that of intimate relationships.

In my own life, some changes have been cumulative, gradual,
and subtle; others have been triggered or intensified by acute epi-
sodes of medical crisis. Without going into the details of my husband's medical history, I will identify and discuss some profound
shifts in my personal and professional attitudes, roles, and beliefs.
These transitions have taken place in response to the life-threaten-
ing experiences of later life, and have somehow coincided with significant events or developments in my professional life.

During my sixtieth year, I completed the work on the first and
only book I have ever co-edited (Robbins & Siegel, 1983). The
publication in November was followed by a most exciting book
party and celebration with my co-editor and several contributors in
San Francisco in mid-January.

Ten days later Ben suffered a serious heart attack. During the
first hours in the local hospital, we had some very quiet and tender
moments of intense intimacy, appreciating the forty years of our
marriage and the glorious vacation we had just spent in Hawaii. We
said good-bye without using the words to say it. The room was clear
and bright in January sunshine, the hospital noises strangely muted,
the fear of death held in abeyance, as the fullness of the lives we
had shared flooded our consciousness. I did not call our children
until later that day when a definite diagnosis had been made and
plans were set in motion for his transfer to the cardiac center of a
nearby town.

Almost automatically, I went into what I call my competent care-
giver mode. I agonized about how to convey the news to our adult
sons and daughter with the least pressure on them. As usual, I was
less cautious with our daughter who had been well trained to be my

ally and automatic helper in the care-giving aspects of our family. Under stress, the feminist rebel in me reverted to the familiar and traditional sex roles and expectations of earlier years.

During the long and tedious days of anxious waiting with other families in the special waiting room for intensive care cardiac patients, I became acutely aware of the precariousness of life, the accidents of fate, and the limits of human intervention and control. The yiddish word *beshert* took on a personal meaning, and my mother's phrase *mazel darf man hoben* kept running through my head. The literal meaning of *beshert* is "that which has been ordained by God." *Mazel* means luck. For me, these phrases out of my childhood expressed an appreciation of the limits of human power and understanding and a profound sense of awe and respect for fate and destiny or the randomness of life.

During Ben's recovery, as I witnessed his depression and the painful adjustment to more limited functioning, I puzzled about how we respond as individuals and as therapists to those aspects of the human condition over which we have little or no control. I noted how much of our energy goes into denying our ultimate powerlessness and into devaluing our valid, adult dependency needs. In the therapy room I now hear more clearly when my clients struggle with similar issues. I now respond with deeper understanding when competent professional women measure themselves against artificial and unrealistic standards of independence and when they are overly critical of their vulnerabilities. I have become aware that the concepts of powerlessness and dependency are associated with gender roles, that they are highly charged emotionally, and that they reflect our cultural values. These issues and observations became the nucleus of a paper on women's "dependency" (Siegel, 1988a).

Two years after Ben's heart attack, and again in the last week of January, he underwent emergency heart by-pass surgery. As I stood by him and witnessed his brave ordeal, it became again an occasion of profound learning for both of us. The surgery was in some ways a more significant emotional turning point than the heart attack had been. The dominant feeling was of hope and the possibility of improvement, as opposed to the feelings of fear and loss during the heart attack. The pre-operative preparation and sharing of information by the cardiac team was such that we both had the opportunity to understand and be impressed with the magnitude of this radical intervention.

This time, when I called our children, I was no longer trying to protect them. Instead I was consciously asking them to be there for me as well as for their father and for their own needs. The roles had shifted. We, the parents, now asked for the emotional support we had previously extended to our now middle-aged children. There was a subtle change in family dynamics, as each of them responded in his or her own way to my new attitude. My self-image had changed. I cried when Judy Eron (1986) sang about aging parents at the Feminist Therapy Institute, seeing myself for the first time as the aging parent, yet sensing that for others the song expressed their feelings as middle-aged daughters.

It has taken me some time to fully realize the impact of this experience. The image that emerges is that of *opening the heart*. It is an image of daring to go to the heart of the matter, be it surgically, intellectually, or emotionally; as applied to creative problem solving, to naming the truth, or to the healing of severe physical or psychological trauma. It is an image that represents tremendous respect for the human capacity to experience injury and to heal.

In my personal life, this has meant a renewed openness to recognizing the potential for change and for new solutions. In my professional life, doing workshops, presentations and writing papers, I grapple more successfully with clarifying and putting new concepts into words and actions. In my therapy practice the effect has been most noticeable in that I can tolerate more of my clients' pain, while the side effects of carrying or witnessing their pain have been greatly reduced. I have sharpened my skills in working with survivors of various kinds of sexual, physical or political abuse. I am learning to trust more deeply, to dare the process of opening my own heart to the pain that we share as women and as human beings, and to do this with less effort. In so doing I am able to convey more hope and confidence to my clients so that they too might take the risk of going to the heart of their pain in order to explore the complex ramifications of their personal scars and to let the healing begin.

This new development in my therapy practice has also involved an examination and clarification of my availability to clients. By combining my new understanding of dependency issues with my expanded ability to tolerate the tensions of painful revelations, I have become more flexible and clearer in setting limits and letting clients know my boundaries.

During these periods of personal crisis, I learned rather painfully that there were only a handful of individuals who were able to respond to my vulnerability without imposing their own mother-transference on me. Far too many friends and family needed me to remain strong and competent at all times. People's gender-role expectations got in the way of the kind of genuine support I could have used. Some of my feminist friends wanted me to remain totally focused on my own needs and professional aspirations, as if my need to be close and supportive to my partner were not also my own need. Most of my more traditional friends and family conveyed surprise and disbelief that anything at all could take me away from my husband at such a time, as if my work were totally unimportant and my constant presence were essential to my husband's recovery.

I felt an increasing sense of loneliness and isolation, as it became clearer to me how very few of my friends were open to talking about the issues that were on my mind. Hardly anyone wanted to hear of illness or death without playing therapist or setting some other distance from me. One of my younger professional friends, who had solicitously asked if I knew how to accept help when I needed it, was frightened and distressed when I cried in front of her, saying, "You're such a role model, it's really hard for me to see you so upset."

The isolation and the receipt of so much ambivalent mother transference refueled my old anger at the double-bind messages that society imposes on women of my generation. After the second world war and through the 1950s, we had been expected to derive great satisfaction from being full-time mothers. During the 1960s, we were accused of overdoing the mothering; the term "momism" entered the mother-blaming vocabulary, and at midlife we dutifully learned to let go of the mothering role. During the 1970s, we became aware of "the problem that has no name" (Friedan, 1963) and "the trauma of eventlessness" (Seidenberg, 1973). At that time some of us were able to move beyond the doldrums and depressions caused by finding our major role so devalued and criticized to develop new interests and create new occupations for ourselves. Now, in the late 1980s, many women my age feel the pressure to give up the work that has given new meaning to our lives. We are now expected to return to volunteering and care-giving.

My old conflict has a new face and a renewed intensity. The pull to return to fulltime homemaking fits in with my occasional longing for more leisure, less structure, and more time for intimacy. The pull to respond to the opportunities for creativity and self-expression that are finally coming my way fits in with my wish to control and structure my own time and to make a meaningful contribution to society while I still have the brain-power and the energy to do it. I experience again a deeply personal conflict leading to yet another transition and a new integration and clarification of my own priorities.

My development as a theorist and practitioner of feminist therapy goes hand in hand with my more personal development as a woman gaining wisdom in old age. My struggle as a woman surviving in a sexist and ageist environment has both informed and been informed by the clarification of ideas and the validation that comes from my interactions with other women, and especially with other feminist writers and therapists. The accommodations my husband and I continue to make to each other are based on more than forty years of caring and sharing, loving and fighting. The limitations that age keeps imposing on our bodies have forced us to become more accepting of our own and each other's imperfections, fears, and sensitivities, but not without occasional eruptions of anger or frustration. We tend to see-saw between feelings of deep appreciation for still being able to enjoy life together, and moments of intense anger and sadness at the many losses of old age. The delights, passions, traumas and doldrums that we continue to experience together continue to deepen the level of trust between us.

This period of transition from midlife to old age has involved a process of significant changes in my innermost being, affecting my most intimate interactions as well as my professional life. Some changes were dramatically initiated by external crisis, others involved a series of moments of awareness and ongoing adaptations in which my personal life was illuminated by my professional reading or by clinical observations of others. Further change and integration of new awareness was facilitated by my efforts to put my observations and ideas into words and to present them in oral or written form.

Two years ago, in an attempt to overcome the growing sense of isolation that I felt in my own community, I initiated the creation of my own support group of women over sixty (Siegel, this volume). A few months later I started a therapy group for older women clients. In these groups we have talked at length about issues that are important to us as older women. I have also begun to collaborate with some older women in making us visible. We are writing about our experiences (Siegel, 1988b; Siegel, in press; Siegel & Sonderegger, in press) and presenting our material at professional conferences.

These activities have plunged me into the world of old women and have helped me overcome my isolation and some of my own age prejudices. I like being with women who have shared the social, cultural and political changes of our generation and who care deeply about what is going on in our world today. Now that I spend more time with older women, I like myself better in my aging body. I have a natural forum for airing the concerns and issues that we have in common and that other friends and colleagues tended to shun. Much of my anger has been channeled into creative energy, and I feel empowered by our association with each other.

REFERENCES

Adelman, M. (Ed.). (1986). *Long time passing: Lives of older lesbians*. Boston, MA: Alyson.
Alexander, J., Berrow, D., Domitrovich, L., Donnelly, M., and McLean, C. (Eds.). (1986). *Women and aging: An anthology by women*. Corvallis, OR: Calyx.
Brecher, E. M. and Editors of Consumers Union (Eds.). (1984). *Love, sex, and aging: A Consumers Union report*. Mount Vernon, NY: Consumers Union.
Butler, R. and Lewis, M. (1976). *Sex after 60*. New York: Harper & Row.
Copper, B. (1988). *Over the hill*. Freedom, CA: Crossing.
Doress, P. B., Siegal, D. L. and The Midlife and Older Women Book Project with The Boston Women's Health Book Collective (Eds.). (1987). *Ourselves, growing older: Women aging with knowledge and power*. New York: Simon & Schuster.

Eron, J. P., (singer-songwriter), (1986). Aging parents. In *Reach across the miles*. (Cassette recording). Nashville, TN: Barleo Records.

Friedan, B. (1963). *The feminine mystique*. New York: Norton.

Macdonald, B., and Rich, C. (1983). *Look me in the eye: Old women, aging and ageism*. San Francisco CA: Spinsters, Ink.

Robbins, J. H., and Siegel, R. J. (1983). *Women changing therapy: New assessments, values, and strategies in feminist therapy*. New York: The Haworth Press.

Seidenberg, R. (1973). The trauma of eventlessness. In J. B. Miller (Ed.), *Psychoanalysis and women* (pp. 350-362). Baltimore: Penguin.

Siegel, R. J. (1988a). Women's "dependency" in a male-centered value system. *Women & Therapy*, 7, 113-123.

Siegel, R. J. (1988b). No longer middle-aged; An integration of personal and professional growth during the therapist's transition to old age. In *Proceedings of the 27th International Conference for the Advancement of Private Practice of Clinical Social Work*. (Available from Roberta Graziano, 146-18 32nd Avenue, Flushing, NY 11354.)

Siegel, R. J. (in press). Old women as mother figures. In E. Cole and J. Knowles (Eds.), *Woman-defined motherhood*. New York: Harrington Park Press.

Siegel, R. J. (this volume). We are not your mothers: Report on two groups for women over sixty.

Siegel, R. J. and Sonderegger, T. B. (in press). Ethical considerations in feminist psychotherapy with women over sixty. In H. Lerman and N. Porter (Eds.), *Ethics in psychotherapy: Feminist perspectives*. New York: Springer.

Walker, B.G. (1985). *The crone*. San Francisco: Harper & Row.

We Are Not Your Mothers: Report on Two Groups for Women Over Sixty

Rachel Josefowitz Siegel, MSW

SUMMARY. A therapist reflects on the isolating effect of ageist stereotyping on women over sixty. She identifies our need to be seen and be heard. She reports on a support group and a therapy group for women over sixty, focusing on group formation, dynamics, communication patterns, and content of discussions.

We are not your mothers, neither are we the mothers you wish you had. We do not want to mother you or smother you. We do not want to repress or devour you. We are neither witch, old hag, or role model, though we can have moments of acting like any or all of these. We feel silenced and invisible when you treat us stereotypically and when you exclude us, ignore us and shy away from our concerns. We need to be seen and heard as individuals. We need to communicate with women who are our own age as well as women who are older and younger than we are.

We want to break down the barriers that ageism places between women. We ask you to look at the feelings and attitudes of middle aged and younger practitioners, teachers, and theoreticians toward old women. How do these feelings affect the younger woman's interactions with older clients, students, colleagues and friends?

The author wishes to thank the Wise Old Women and the members of the therapy group for all the ways they have participated in this report.

Presented at Association for Women in Psychology Annual Meeting, Denver, CO, March 1987.

Reprints available from Rachel Josefowitz Siegel, 108 W Buffalo St., Ithaca, NY 14850.

What is the impact of these feelings and attitudes on the topics we do or do not discuss at professional meetings and feminist conferences, and the articles we do or do not write about women of all ages? Barbara Macdonald (1986) has noted the silence that surrounds old women and their issues in the field of women's studies. Nancy Chodorov and Susan Contrato (1982) have commented on the invisibility of the mother's perspective in mother/daughter feminist literature. Such biases and lack of information about old women limit our understanding of all women and interfere with optimal academic and clinical work. These silences and invisibilities also cause our own aging to be problematic and isolated.

In this paper we will break the silence by reporting on a support group and a therapy group for women over sixty, and we will start by placing these groups within the context of the ageist environment that forms the background of our experiences as old women.

A LOOK AT OUR OWN AGEISM

No matter how old we are, older women evoke in each of us very primitive and powerful feelings about the woman (or women) who mothered us, and about the woman we will become as we age. We try to escape from these feelings by keeping our distance, making older women invisible, or by rigidifying old women into positively idealized role models or negatively caricatured stereotypes. We often fall back into ambivalent modes of mother/daughter interactions. When we respond to old women as mother figures, feeling intimidated by their imagined power and control over us, or resenting their real or imagined dependency on us, we activate our own fears of being overprotected and disempowered or of becoming as helpless as they appear to us. We see in them the prototypes and conveyors of gender limitations imposed by our society on all women. Since we are all still struggling to move out of these restrictive roles and redefine our own capabilities on our own terms, we tend to avoid the women who remind us of the helpless dependency and nurturing self-lessness that society devalues and would reduce us to.

We who are old and we who will be old all carry in our own heads a male-centered ambivalence toward mothers and a male-oriented, youth-worshipping fear of aging. These feelings, when they remain unexamined, cause us to avoid and oppress older women and to distort the aging process within ourselves. Some of us have found that our relationships with all women have been enriched by working on these issues with our own mothers or daughters, directly or in therapy or women's groups.

No woman can grow up in our society without learning to pass, attempting to look and feel younger. As we get older, the pressure to appear younger increases:

> Somewhere in our fifties, the mass of anxieties about age, and the increase of rejection and invisibility we experience, becomes critical. This is often the time when our trained inability to identify with women older than ourselves reaches its climax. Old women cannot rely upon the midlife woman as ally. The midlife woman, in her rage and fear, may unconsciously discharge all kinds of covert aggression against the old woman as the personification of what is threatening her. (Copper, 1986, pp. 47-48)

During my own progression from midlife to the beginning of old age, I became aware of a gradually increasing gap between myself and my younger colleagues and friends. Though we continued to interact on many levels, I could no longer comfortably share some important aspects of my life. The exclusions and avoidances became more frequent and more painful. I felt angry and isolated. In the summer of 1986 when I attended a workshop for old and older women led by Shevy Healey at the National Women's Studies Association meeting, I discovered the relief and support that a group of my own contemporaries can provide for each other. I came home determined to create such a group in my own community. My first step was to enlist a seventy year old friend in the planning of this new project.

THE SUPPORT GROUP OR, AMONG OURSELVES

Our first decision in the planning of this group was to make decisions on the basis of our own needs. Since we are both therapists, we wanted to be free of that role in this group. We wished to interact with non-therapists and we were determined that this become a group in which the role of facilitator was shared by all.

Our initial criteria for membership were women over sixty, who were not our clients, who would stimulate and interest us, who did not appear needier than we at the moment, and who had a capacity for self-reflection and a willingness or openness to expressing their feelings. We met initially with a nucleus of six women who then participated equally in shaping the group.

We are now thirteen women who have all had some prior acquaintance with each other. Our ages range from 60 to 84. We are aware of our own privileges and that we are not typical of all women over sixty. All but one of us are white; we are all middle class, well educated, and assume the advantages of a heterosexual life style. We are still active in our professional, academic, creative, or community volunteer capacities. We consider ourselves in reasonably good health, although most of us are coping with some moderate to severe health conditions. Each of us has worked or still works outside the home. All but one have been married once; one woman has been married twice, divorced and widowed. Seven are widowed, one is divorced and five still married.

We meet every two weeks in someone's home, bring our own lunch and talk without a predetermined agenda. During our first session we very quickly agreed that our focus would be on our own aging and that we would have no facilitator or leader. While we acknowledged that some of us would be out of town for prolonged periods, each of us made a sincere commitment to attend regularly when in town. We also decided that we would talk freely to others about the group, but would respect each other's privacy by not revealing personal comments or information about any particular woman in the group.

At our first meeting, we named ourselves WOW! Wise Old Women.

Our meetings have been stimulating and the content of our discussions often deeply moving, steadily liberating and supportive, and sometimes specifically helpful in providing information, suggestions and group support in particular situations. Attendance is steady and enthusiasm continues to be high.

What do we talk about?

Early on we discovered the commonality of shared local history and the pleasures of being with women who had lived through the same political, cultural, ideological and economic changes and events.

We began and have often returned to the topic of death and final illness—our own, our parents', our partner's, spouse's, friends', children's. We have shared our concerns about planning for catastrophic illness or the gradual loss of our capacities; about how we will manage when we can no longer drive, or need more personal or nursing care. We have talked about living wills to protect us from prolonged and intrusive medical interventions when we can no longer express our own wishes, and we have talked about euthanasia.

We have discussed what we will leave behind and how to do it: the legal and financial aspects of aging, insurance, wills; the passing on of family and personal history, photographs, letters, diaries or journals, meaningful objects, and we have examined how we know what is worth saving and meaningful and to whom.

We sensed an early tension between wanting to focus on matters of death and dying on the one hand, and matters of life on the other. Our need to talk of death, dying, and loss of function seemed intensified by our awareness that these topics were shunned in other settings.

We have talked in some detail about housing, and how and whether we could create our own communal living unit with nursing care. We talk about wanting to remain independent and in control of our own life and health decisions. We try to anticipate and make plans for the possibility of becoming dependent on others for our physical care. In response to my questioning the values implied by our fear of dependency, we have begun to explore what the term means to us. The group is a safe place to talk about physical impairments such as loss of hearing and visual acuity, cataract operations, circulatory problems, difficulties with walking and driving at night, and lapses of memory. Some of us have talked about cutting back on our work and enjoying more leisure and less stress. We have talked about travel, vacations, and entertainment, and how we feel about doing things alone and living alone or how we feel about the time we spend with our partners and with our children.

We reminisce about the social climate of earlier years, our own changes, our own contributions to our community, and the delays and interruptions of our careers. We live in a college town and have noticed that most of us enjoy the company of younger people. We appreciate the contributions of younger generations, and share many of their concerns and enthusiasms about social and political changes. We continue to be personally and actively involved in creating such changes, but we have some difficulties with current media of expression, the multimedia bombardment of the senses and high noise levels.

We have talked about incidents of age prejudice and of being invisible among younger people, without labeling these events as ageism. We have noted that for some of us this group is a shift to enjoying and seeking out the company of older women. We talk of loneliness, but not of intimacies. We have shared some of our personal and professional histories, anecdotes of childhood and adolescence as well as our early or current political concerns and involvements.

We have intense discussions on a variety of broader women's issues, along with current politics and community affairs. We do not always agree. We are beginning to explore our differences, having at first focused primarily on our commonalities.

We are comfortably using the communication patterns of our generation. We don't spill our guts, yet we are sensitive to innuendo; on the whole we are direct, but careful to respect each other's privacy, and to avoid intrusion.

There are deep and long-lasting friendships within the group, as well as subgroups and overlapping relationships. Intimate matters are undoubtedly shared outside of group meetings. Group discussions have opened up topics not previously dealt with within the existing relationships.

The group is now in its third year. We have begun to be more open about the more private and sensitive issues of religion, sex, sexuality, or sexual preference. We have celebrated together and mourned together. We have helped each other through illness and medical treatments. We laugh a lot and we express good feelings about each other.

THE THERAPY GROUP

Empowered by my participation in the support group, I sent out a flyer announcing a therapy group for older women. Within a very short time, five women had signed up. This group met as a therapy group for about eight months, during which time I maintained the role of facilitator. This group also was white, middle class, and well educated; members were either still employed, about to be retired, or active in post-retirement occupations. The age range was 60 to 65. Communication patterns were similar in both groups with respect to privacy and early avoidance of sexuality.

The initial mood of the group was mildly depressed, with a low energy level, slow tempo and much hesitation about revealing problem areas. By joining the group, each member had acknowledged that she had some worrisome concerns to work on. A brainstorming session during the second meeting identified the following topics in the order in which the group wanted to address them. Though some issues were of particular interest to only one woman, there was general consensus about priorities:

1. Living without a job — managing money and time, feeling useful and needed, finding goals or purpose, having fun, improving and enjoying a social life.
2. Accepting the changes of aging — sorting out hopes and dreams, getting along with elderly parents, adult children and friends, adjusting to the distance of grown children.
3. Planning for the future — evaluating new living arrangements, planning for possible disability, making funeral plans.

The therapy group paid more attention to problem solving and coping strategies. Concerns were aired about the transition to retirement and the resulting changes in daily patterns and routines. Anger was expressed at incidents of age discrimination in the workplace which made retirement more problematic. Group members shared their feelings about the care of aging parents and their sense of ambivalence regarding their own aging bodies.

Each woman dealt in her own way with the recurrent theme of making life meaningful outside of the structure of paid employment and finding ways of valuing what we do in later life when there is no obvious outside recognition of it. Another theme for each woman was that of respecting who she was — her body, her interests, the skills she was now using in new contexts. Members had difficulty giving themselves credit for their own activities and ongoing accomplishments, while they were impressed by each other's achievements.

In the therapy group, we paid attention to the anxiety, depression and anger that emerged in the discussions of death, illness, nursing home care, and financial insecurities. Some women recognized a high level of stress and powerlessness about the unknown quality of their future health and about not knowing when or how each of us will die.

During my winter vacation, the therapy group met without a facilitator. The members reported that they felt empowered by this experience, but not quite ready to continue on their own. Four months later, however, the therapy group transformed itself into a leaderless support group and have been meeting without me ever since.

CONCLUDING REMARKS

The topics of discussion in both groups have been remarkably similar but the emotional tone and energy levels have differed. Both groups have participated since the beginning in giving me feedback and suggestions for this report. Both groups have expressed good feelings and some excitement at sharing our experiences with a wider audience and becoming visible and vocal about our aging process.

It is my sense that we are not only exploring our own issues in both groups, but that we are also recognizing and moving beyond our own ageism, learning to appreciate ourselves and each other more fully as old women in an environment that devalues us as we get older. We too have absorbed the ageist messages of our environment and they are getting in our way. We need supportive environments in which we can hear and be heard, support and be supported, nurture and be nurtured in an equal and interdependent fashion.

We are trying to be ourselves and groping for our own answers.

We need some space and time that is free of mother expectations, free of nurturing others one-sidedly, and free of ageist and sexist devaluation or idealization. We are trying to live fully by integrating the knowledge of death into our lives. We are making what we can out of the years or days still left to us.

REFERENCES

Chodorov, N. & Contrato, S. (1982). The fantasy of the perfect mother. In B. Thorne and M. Yalom (Eds.), *Rethinking the family: Some feminist questions* (pp. 54-71). New York: Longman.

Copper, B. (1986). Voices: On becoming old women, In J. Alexander, D. Berrow, L. Domitrovich, M. Donnelly, and C. McLean (Eds.), *Women and aging: An anthology by women* (pp. 47-48). Corvalis, OR: Calyx.

Macdonald, B. (1986). Outside the sisterhood: Ageism in Women's Studies. In J. Alexander, D. Berrow, L. Domitrovich, M. Donnelly and C. McLean. (Eds.), *Women and aging: An anthology by women* (pp. 20-25). Corvalis, OR: Calyx.

At Sixty-One

Like a panther
age crept up on me

but I refuse
to conform to its stereotype

instead will plunge forward
in my endeavors

nourish and stretch my mind
with new concepts,
thoughts, ideas

share knowledge
with my students,
neighbors, friends.

The panther gives me strength.

—Ingrid Reti

Extended Care-Giving:
The Experience of Surviving Spouses

Sandra L. Quinn-Musgrove, PhD

SUMMARY. For the most part, care-giving is a function expected, even demanded, by terminally ill spouses, their families, and friends. This paper includes a brief introduction to issues surrounding care-giving, a fictionalized story of a long term care-giver, and interviews with ten women and two men who served as care-givers. The care-givers read the story and responded to it in terms of their own experiences. Their stories are reported here to illuminate the care-giving role as seen by care-givers themselves.

INTRODUCTION

By the mid-1980s, life expectancy of Americans neared 80 years for women and 72 for men. The number of Americans over 65 climbed to 26.8 million, or more than 11 percent of the total population. By the year 2030, almost 20 percent of all Americans will be over the age of 65 (Schaefer, 1986).

These figures are not news, having been accurately projected almost a generation ago. The news is our increasing recognition that we face the future with few means available or planned to provide "quality-life" for old people. Of particular interest to me is the failure, by all sectors of society, to confront issues associated with care-givers—those persons charged with responsibility for the soci-

Sandra L. Quinn-Musgrove, currently Assistant Professor of political science and public administration at Our Lady of the Lake University in San Antonio, TX, chairs the Department of Social Studies there. She earned her doctorate in political science from Claremont and has published widely on American government and higher education. Prior to entering college as a freshman in 1973, she held management positions in retail merchandising for fifteen years.

ological, financial, physiological, and psychological concerns of terminally ill family members, particularly spouses.

Because women generally outlive males, and because tradition dictates that wives will "naturally" serve as care-givers, many middle aged and old women spend their lives as care-givers to husbands suffering from increasingly debilitating illnesses. The end of life for the terminally ill spouse too often indicates the care-giver's giving up on life as well.

Commonly, the duration of a spouse's long term illness has raised havoc with, if not destroyed, the physiological and psychological resources of the care-giver. Physical and emotional stress experienced by care-givers are regularly overlooked, ignored, or even accepted as normal by family and friends. During long term terminal illness, both patient and care-giver regularly experience social isolation, and the longer the illness, the more isolated both become.

From my own experience as a care-giver, and the experiences of several others interviewed by me, I synthesized in fictional form a surviving spouse's story. In individual sessions and one focus group session, I used the story as a stimulus for a dozen care-givers to reflect on their own experiences.

METHODOLOGY

A brief explanation of the subject was given prior to the interview. I anticipated that some individuals might reject further examination of the subject of care-giver, but once the explanation was given, only one person demurred. The candidate for interview, a woman, then went on to explain her anger about the subject. This care-giver's experiences were omitted from my report. Each interviewee read the story with me present, and I conducted the interview session immediately afterward. In each instance, I gave assurance of confidentiality, and edited the interviews to protect confidentiality and avoid repetition.

I do not propose that the story, or the interviews, represent fully the experiences of all care-givers. Certainly, such a study would be possible, but much universality of care-giver experiences is, I believe, apparent even in this brief interview series. With the exception of the individual cited above, who declined my request, all individuals approached were interviewed. For the individual interviews, held over a three-month period, I requested the interview once I discovered the person was a widow. The single group meeting was conducted with a widow/widower support group. Relevant interviewee characteristics are summarized in Table 1.

I did not intend to shock the care-givers who read "The Silenced Death," and I was not disappointed. However, I was caught short by my own visceral reaction to the unleashed emotions expressed to me by some of those who read the story. In this case truth was stronger than fiction.

THE SILENCED DEATH: A FICTIONALIZED ACCOUNT OF A SURVIVING SPOUSE

On February 12, 1956, she celebrated her fortieth birthday. Though contrived youthfulness had yet to capture the attention of the nation's maturing citizens, Marilyn Converse looked younger than her years. Her eyes sparkled with laughter, though crinkles at the corners had begun to make faint etchings. From her only slightly dulling, natural, auburn hair, to slender ankles—often encircled by straps of shoes popular in the fifties—her personality projected exuberance.

Marilyn's life was full. With pleasurable anticipation, she looked to the future with Raymond, her husband of twenty-two years.

In the darkness of early morning hours, the telephone rang.

Long accustomed to sleeping alone during months when Raymond worked alternating shifts on the railroad, Marilyn woke, sleep-walking to the kitchen telephone and lifted the receiver.

"Hello, Mrs. Converse?"

Sleepily, Marilyn answered "Yes" and asked, "Who's calling?"

"This is St. Joseph's Hospital. The Emergency Room."

Now fully awake, and conscious of the fear she felt invade her voice, she asked "Is something wrong?"

"Your husband, Raymond, is in the Emergency Room. Could you come to the hospital?"

Table 1: Characteristics of Care-givers

NAME*	PRESENT AGE	AGE AT ON-SET	SPOUSE AGE AT ON-SET	DURATION OF ILLNESS	DISEASE	STATUS OF PATIENT
Frank	64	59	53	3 yrs.	Cancer	Deceased
James	73	64	61	8 yrs.	Stroke	Deceased
Eve	67	50	52	14 yrs.	Various	Deceased
Joanne	69	49	57	8 yrs.	Emphysema**	Deceased
Irma	72	40	43	21 yrs.	Accident**	Deceased
Marilyn	66	57	65	2 yrs.	Heart	Deceased
Sara	57	51	56	6 mos.	Cancer	Deceased
Lenore	52	33	50	15 yrs.	Cancer	Survived #
Carol	57	47	62	10 yrs.	Altzheimer's	Living
Ann	53	36	40	16 yrs.	Cancer**	Living
Susan	36	29	32	-0-	Accident	Deceased
Rose	49	47	51	-0-	Heart	Deceased

* The real names of all persons included in this paper have been changed.

** The disease at the time of identification was already advanced, and though the patient survived, other diseases are added to the initial diagnosis.

\# At present the original diagnosis is in remission; however numerous other diseases have been added to an extended list of illnesses experienced by this patient.

"I'll be there as soon as I can," and she hung up the telephone, breathed in deeply, and again lifted the receiver.

Though early, Marilyn's immediate thought was to contact her two daughters. She called each.

"Dad has been hurt. I'm on my way to the hospital. No, you don't need to come. Stay with the children, and I'll call you as soon as I know more."

Her optimism, though tempered by fear, allowed her to tell each daughter, "You'll see him tomorrow at home. I'm sure he'll be able to come home. Either way, I'll let you know. I'm sure he'll be all right, or they wouldn't have called me that way!"

Marilyn dressed and drove to the hospital.

She was right. Raymond survived. But little by little, crinkle to line, laughter to anger, and love to pain, Marilyn died. On April 23, 1975, twenty years after the accident, her husband ceased breathing. The twenty years cost Marilyn her life.

Raymond's death began when a train engine threw him over a telephone pole. A series of increasingly debilitating illnesses followed, gradually eroding both his mind and body to such a condition that when death finally came, those at his funeral pronounced "It was a blessing."

Twenty years after the 1956 telephone call, Marilyn stood by Raymond's casket, listening to further whispers of condolence. Her two daughters stood at her side.

In 1976, Marilyn stood slightly bent, her grayed hair pulled back and brushed into an unkempt, knotted bun, appropriate for a woman of her years. Though tears moistened her eyes, there was little life in the blue iris, and their circles were wedged deeply among the lines that ravaged her face. Among themselves, others whispered:

"It's been hard on Marilyn."

"She's a good woman."

Others, less understanding, commented:

"She looks so old doesn't she?"

"She can't be much out of her sixties, is she?"

They distanced themselves from the widow.

Standing still, as family and the few remaining friends passed and whispered to Marilyn and her daughters, she thought of the two decades just ended. Each daughter dutifully called, and occasionally visited, serving to, as they defined it, ". . . take the load off Mom." Though one daughter had moved across country, calls and occasional visits continued.

"How's Dad?"

"He's eating a little more this week."

"The doctor said he can begin to use a walker."

"The stroke has affected his personality."

Finally, the litany of Raymond's illnesses neared an end with "The cancer has metasticized to his brain."

In the months immediately preceding his death, the girls' calls came more frequently, punctuated by increased visits. Only days before Raymond was admitted to the hospital for the final stay,

Marilyn's older daughter came to stay, explaining "I'll take over now, Mom. You need some rest."

This morning, on the way to the funeral for her husband, each daughter lovingly told Marilyn "Now, Mom, you begin to live your life. Dad would have wanted it that way. You deserve it."

Marilyn thought "Now I can begin my life?" In a silenced, twenty-year-old scream, she raged "Why did it end twenty years ago?"

At sixty, Marilyn was bitter, aged, and angry. Her loss had not occurred when Raymond died. Her loss began as the doctor pronounced, months after the train accident, "He'll never regain either mental or physical function that will allow him to live a normal, full life."

Marilyn had listened quietly, unaware that at that moment her own, silenced death began.

As the line passing the casket ended, Marilyn stood by herself; others in the room kept their distance, viewing, they believed, the grieving widow.

She remembered dinners unshared with friends, family, or husband. The few outings she took, alone. Soon she became isolated, forced into a land between married and single. It was expected. Marilyn was a married widow. There was no socially acceptable escape without publicly rejecting the promise of the pronouncement on their wedding day, ". . . for better or worse."

Bitterness grew. This day, as her eyes teared, she knew the tears were not caused by sorrow of Raymond's death. Instead, her tears were a public expression of twenty years of anger, though words remained unspoken.

One of Raymond's rarely seen cousins stopped to whisper, "You took such good care of him. He looks wonderful." Marilyn's stomach turned in rage.

Five years after the accident, Marilyn considered leaving Raymond. She knew someone, somewhere, would take care of him. She read a story about a husband leaving his wife, upon learning about the permanency of a crippling accident. The true story quoted the man as saying "I'm young, and I have a right to a full life." Yet, to Marilyn, and she knew the same could be said of her family and friends, the implications of the story were clear. "How" the story asked, "could a husband leave his wife only because she could no longer be his wife, share his pleasures, love, laugh, and walk with him?"

Though the story tempted her, Marilyn knew that public castigations, real or unspoken, were more than she could face. She would appear weak and a failure. She stayed. The years dragged on.

Only weeks after the funeral, Marilyn spent days with women who were also widowed. "The girls" got together to have fun. Marilyn was again pained, by the hopeless attempts at fun. Each woman desperately sought to recapture lost youth by enticing some new male to enter their lives. Some few of the widows "fortunate to have had husbands who died quickly" Marilyn thought, relished the experiences. More often than not only these women were successful in captivating the infrequent, emotionally stable, older male.

Marilyn was embarrassed. Then hopeless. By 1977 she withdrew back into the world she had lived for twenty years. She isolated herself, though without even the smothering company of a dying husband.

On December 22, 1978, Marilyn Converse ceased breathing from a self-inflicted gunshot. Family and friends consoled each other.

"She couldn't live any longer without Raymond."

"You know, she's been in declining health ever since his death."

"Did you know she was only sixty-two years old?"

"Remember how beautiful she was when she was young?"

In the twenty years it took Raymond to finally, officially, die, Marilyn lost her life. She was not allowed to live, though initially there was nothing to inhibit her experiencing a full emotional and physical life.

But, conscious of public expectations, she silenced her pain and embarked on commitment to her own martyred death.

After Raymond's burial, Marilyn's daughters said,

"Go out, Mom."

"Live it up!"

"It's your turn now."

But, it was too late.

THE EXPERIENCES
OF CARE-GIVING REMEMBERED

Q: What is your general response to "The Silenced Death"?

A: *Eve:* I can appreciate what it says. I can't say my experience was exactly the same, but the general tone fit very well. Mine lasted 14 years. My husband was senile during that time, and it was difficult to take care of him. He wouldn't cooperate. During that time I lost most friends. I did work though, and at least I could escape during the day. On week-ends, I lived in isolation.

Ann: I feel like that woman is me, except my husband just keeps on living. He goes from one disease to another. For years I've thought "this" will be the one that finally ends it — but it never does. It just keeps going on, and on, . . . I've gotten to the point I think he's immortal. I'm convinced he'll outlive me because of the constant stress. I know it sounds terrible, but really it's good to talk to someone I think understands. I went to counseling for two years [five years earlier] and I don't really know if it helped or not. Mostly every day I go home from work angry.

Lenore: I'm afraid that would have been me, if I didn't leave him! I still support him, and frankly that makes me mad too. He was "dying" three separate times. By the third time, I didn't want him to recover. Every time he'd get a cold, he'd threaten me — or it seemed like a threat — "I've got the big 'C' again." I can't imagine what I'd have done if I'd stayed, and he did get it again.

Sara: Mine was different. It only lasted six months. I thought to be thankful for the time we had together. I don't know how it would have been if he'd survived all those years. I do know it was constant stress. I just don't know. . . .

Q: Compared to the longer term illnesses, do you think you would have been able to maintain your attitude of relative acceptance?

A: *Sara:* I think I'd have been worn out. He had been healthy, and we had an active life. It's different, I think.

A: *Joanne:* For the last eight years, he sat here [a group met at her home] in this chair with an oxygen tank behind us — behind him. I was constantly on the alert because I realized he needed oxygen all of the time. He was mobile, a lot of the time, but I never knew when he was going to have a, I won't call it a seizure—but with emphysema just all of a sudden he'd quit breathing, and I would work resuscitating him. I was afraid to go off and leave him. If I did, I'd worry about getting back. It was just constant. It was fear and guilt. Back and forth!

Q: What do you mean 'guilt'?

A: *Joanne:* I guess I mean that I thought if he died, whether or not I was there, that it would be my fault.

Ann: I don't really feel guilty about the illness anymore, but I feel guilty about wishing he would die, and about the problems the children have, and sometimes about my constant escaping to work, leaving him alone, and liking it!

Frank: The thing with me was, I guess, blaming myself for certain things that took place. She went into a coma, I guess it was, and I remember going in and trying to slap her. But, I'd forgotten she was on [a blood thinner], and all you had to do was just look at her and she turned blue. She had blue marks all over her. I got scared and called the EMS. I told 'em what happened. Things like that got involved. I wasn't ever sure if I was doing the right thing. The only child we had was about thirty-five at the time, an adopted son [later clarified as her son adopted by Frank]—he committed suicide about a year after she died. I still worry if I did something wrong, and that's why he killed himself. Shortly after she died, I went out and bought myself a computer. I'd been interested in them for years, and couldn't afford one. My son came over, and I felt real guilty 'cause I'd spent the money. I don't know.

Q: Where were your families at the time of the illnesses?

A: *Eve:* Our son lives in another city. He had a great deal of difficulty dealing with it. When my husband went to the hospital he came and tried to deal with it. But, he just wanted to remove himself. He didn't call very often. I guess he mostly just didn't want to call and hear me say the same things over and over. But, one of the times he came back—I just never saw or heard anyone more gentle than he was with his father . . .

Joanne: I have a son and a daughter. I still almost never see my son, even though he lives right here. While his Dad was sick, he showed up, but nothing was ever right. I don't know if he still blames me for his death.

Ann: My daughter was sixteen at the time he first got sick. She ran away. Eight months later she showed up; she was on heroin for ten years. She's off it now, but really there's little contact. Our son was only about seven when he first got diagnosed. When he was twelve he lost all of his hair. The doctors said it was stress and nerves. He had to take care of his Dad a lot, because I was working. He's never gotten hair back. He really never recovered, and his Dad still keeps after him. It's constant. No matter what he does, it's wrong!

Q: What about friends?

A: *Frank:* Some of the friends I had, I didn't want. We didn't have a lot of friends before, but a cousin came over to the house — she was a super-religious person — and started praying with my wife, and she started crying. It made me mad! This was way early in the track, before she even got very serious.

Ann: Friends were only good for the short run. Even really good friends got tired of listings of all the symptoms. He used to tell everyone all about all his symptoms, no matter how intimate they were, and then if a friend responded with some illness they had, it just wasn't important. Theirs didn't compare to the "big 'C'."

Eve: The longer the disease went on, the fewer people came over. Outside of work, I just had no friends. It was like they forgot.

James: She couldn't talk anyway. At first people used to come over, but I guess 'cause I was always busy, it seems like, pretty soon almost everyone did stop coming over, or even calling. I did have one couple that came over a lot, . . . brought food on Sundays. Then I found the man was "borrowing" stuff from my garage shop. I didn't know it — I guess he took it when I'd be busy — and then I found out, confronted him, and he told me I didn't need it anyway, 'cause I had to take care of her. That's the last I ever saw them.

Eve: I think the friends we had were frightened by the ongoing illness. It was sort of like looking at their own mortality.

Q: Most of you have spoken about guilt. What about anger?

A: *Ann*: Mostly because of the counseling, I guess it helped there, I can admit that I'm mad. It seems like I have a right to be mad, but I'm not supposed to show it, or even admit it—certainly not to anyone!

Joanne: At the time I wasn't angry, but several years later the anger—not too long ago in fact—I just got so mad!

Frank: Men aren't supposed to get angry because a woman is sick with something she didn't cause. Now I know I was really angry. I remember her vanity. After she had the chemo-therapy, she needed to wear a wig. She spent hours with those damn wigs. I wanted to throw 'em at her. I was just so busy, and all she could think about were the wigs! God!

James: I wasn't exactly a kid when she got sick, and we'd had a pretty good life up until that time. Then that bloody stroke. I didn't have any kind of life, and here she was, didn't seem to know what was going on. Sometimes I'd go and stomp around the ranch, just so I could get the anger out. I knew I was mad, but didn't want her to see it.

Q: Did you consider leaving your spouse during the illness?

A: *James:* No, I didn't. I just couldn't see what would be done with her. We didn't have any children, so I didn't have to answer to them. I just didn't dare leave. But, there were times when I'd see her laying in the hospital bed at home, and I just wished I wasn't or she wasn't there. Early on after she had the stroke, I had sex with the lady I hired to help me with her. Right there in the same house. I can't say it was an affair, but I gave her one of [his wife's] rings. She used to wear it right in front of [his wife]. I kind of worried if she ever said anything to her.

Ann: I think about leaving him all of the time, even now. I had an affair that lasted two years. It wasn't very good, but I thought that maybe someone else might be available if I wasn't so obviously tied to a sick man. Now if I left, I'd lose everything. What court would award me the house or any of the things that have accumulated? Now I'll just stick it out. It's him or me.

Lenore: I did leave him. He's still alive. I still support him, but he's gone to live with one of the children. He seems quite happy. He's just waiting for another attack, I guess. I wish I'd done it earlier. I really don't have any regrets, but it sure did cause comments by some of the people I knew. Actually it was worse than that. Some people completely ostracized me — but, it's not much different than when he was sick for the long times. This time the ostracization is just for a different reason.

(Carol, quoted below, learned her husband's illness was Alzheimer's disease, approximately ten years ago.)

Q: What was your first reaction when you heard the identity of the disease?

A: *Carol:* Actually, I didn't react much at all. Then, Alzheimer's was just barely known. It's only been in the last few years that it's become "popular." At first both of us saw it as an opportunity to be together for a lot of time. We had all these plans, which we instituted. We bought an RV; my husband retired, and I made plans to work periodically (she is a professional fund-raiser, free lance). We just planned to spend time, whatever it was, traveling, and then periodically returning home to visit the doctor and children.

Q: Now, ten years later, you're still on the road. (Our RVs were parked next to each other in an RV park.) How do you feel about the last 10 years?

A: *Carol:* The first few years it was really quite good. He was able to ride, converse quite a bit, and we really enjoyed our life. About three years ago, I found I had to work more to support our lifestyle. We'd sold our home to purchase the first RV. This is our first time out for almost eight months, and it's the last time. I just can't do anything with him anymore. (Her husband was sitting passively at the picnic table as the interview was conducted.) I can't leave him alone for a minute. He doesn't know where he is or what he or anyone else is doing. It's like taking care of a great big baby!

Q: How do your children feel about the nomadic lifestyle you've had for these years?

A: *Carol:* At first they liked it — thought it was a good idea. But, now, this time I decided to take this trip, they are furious at me. Our son accused me of trying to kill him! I don't know . . ., maybe he's right. Anyway, we're on our way back to Oklahoma now. I'll just have to face them when we get home. I don't know how I'll handle it from now on.

(Rose and Susan, quoted below, were in the group interview. Their husbands died of a heart attack and accident, respectively.)

Q: What circumstances preceded your husband's death?

A: *Rose:* My husband had a heart attack in '79, but he seemed all right physically, sort of, until he died. Except, he changed psychologically after the heart attack. I'd gotten used to the change, but about a year before he died I'd gotten mad at him, quite a bit actually, because he refused to take care of himself. He always said "I'll have a heart attack and leave you. You can take care of yourself. You've got a job. You don't have to worry about anything." Then I'd feel guilty, but I was angry at him a lot because he wouldn't take care of himself. Keep his weight down, exercise, and all that kind of thing. I felt like he was ready to leave me. He gave up.

Q: After his death, what was your reaction?

A: *Rose:* I was numb for about three months. I didn't want to talk or anything.

Q: Did guilt enter into your pre-death or post-death reactions?

A: *Rose:* Only sometimes there was guilt, but I think he resolved to die. I don't know why. He didn't have any visible physical problems. I tried to get him to take care of himself, but. . . .

Q: Your husband died in a ship accident. Your reaction?

A: *Susan:* My husband was just 32 when he died. I was pregnant and 29. I wasn't angry then, but I find now I'm angry quite a bit.

Q: How did your friends react to your husbands' deaths?

A: *Susan:* I called our two best friends, and asked them to come over. They really never left my side during all of the arrangements. They're still good friends today. We see each other frequently.

Rose: I guess they were like all friends. Some helped. All expressed sympathy, and some of them I see regularly, while others. . . .

Q: What is your reaction, as a widow, to "The Silenced Death"?

A: *Rose:* I can't say that I experienced the trials she went through, but, there was anger. Though its source was different. One thing apparent to me was the recovery time. It didn't take long to return to a normal life, once my grieving was done. How could anyone live like that, and then return to normal—whatever that is—after all those years?

Susan: Outside of the anger I've recently experienced, after all those years it amazes me. I had friends that supported me, and still do. Nevertheless, as a widow I can and can not imagine the terrible times she must have had.

The individual as Irma in Table 1, is the model for the woman identified as Marilyn Converse in "The Silenced Death." Irma did not literally commit suicide. The metaphorical quality of the story does, however, indicate the quality of life that Irma leads today.

Irma has closed her doors to the world, including having only infrequent contact with her family. She lives in the world; but is not of the world. She has, effectively, committed social suicide, and views herself as "only existing until I stop breathing." It is appropriate to observe that Irma today is reliving years experienced with her husband. One interviewee observed of Marilyn Converse, "She chose to die."

CONCLUSION

The experiences of illness, aging, and care-giving presented here will expand, clamoring for public response in the near future. There are other related issues that need to be addressed in both the private and public sectors, such as the financial responsibility for long term care of aged or diseased people. But, the emotional and physical quality of life of care-givers is not yet on the public agenda and in private is spoken of in muted, infrequent whispers.

We have not moved far from the care-giving era of ". . . for better or worse" when we review and consider the responsibility with full accountability that long term care-givers must experience, for the most part, in silence and isolation. In years to come, when one of five adults is aged, and when women will continue to be charged with the care-giver role because of the likelihood of outliving their husbands, will we continue to permit private lives and thoughts to produce social, emotional, or physical suicide? It is time we place the issues surrounding long term care-giving on the public agenda, and confront openly the private pain of care-giving.

Duologue

for Polly on her 58th birthday

From the moment you arrive
we careen recklessly
through the intellectual landscape

words swirl
like wind whipped leaves

the topics flare
literature, poetry, politics,
sexism, ageism

opinions burst forth
the room boils with ideas

we share, agree, disagree
stimulate each other
to glowing exhaustion.

—Ingrid Reti

Reflections of Midlife Lesbians
on Their Adolescence

Barbara E. Sang, PhD

SUMMARY. A group of 110 midlife lesbians filled out several open-ended essay questions on adolescence and midlife. Half the sample described themselves as non-traditional adolescents, e.g., bookish, rebellious or athletic. Approximately half the midlife lesbians had non-traditional dreams in adolescence, that is dreams of careers, adventure and having an impact on the world. Women who labeled themselves as "lesbians" in their teens and twenties were more likely to have been non-traditional adolescents. Women who labeled themselves as "lesbians" in midlife were more traditional as adolescents. The majority of lesbians in this sample were highly educated professional women. The data suggested that adolescent dreams and interests served as a source of vitality and creativity for midlife lesbians.

Middle-aged women of today grew up at a time when it was difficult for women to use their potential. It is no wonder that several contemporary studies of midlife women show them to be searching for an identity independent of husbands and children (Junge & Maya, 1985; Lopata & Barnewolt, 1984; Rubin, 1979). Women of this generation were promised self-fulfillment if they gave up their own lives to meet the needs of others. Midlife transition for these women is often filled with turmoil and self-doubt as

Barbara E. Sang is a clinical psychologist in private practice in New York City. Since 1968 she has been active in the gay and women's movements. She is a member of Creative Explorations: Artist Therapy Service.

This research is part of a larger study on "Existential Issues of Midlife Lesbians" which will appear in an anthology tentatively titled, *Getting Better: Lesbians at Midlife* (Sang, Smith & Warshow). This project was funded by the author.

111

old roles are being shed and the shape of new ones were not apparent (Rubin, 1979).

Middle-aged women have been examined from a heterosexual perspective, but not from a lesbian perspective. Because lesbians as a group have rejected the traditional role stereotypes of what females were supposed to be, I hypothesized that they would have been freer to develop their individual potential with respect to career and special interests and that their non-conformity would be reflected in the kinds of life issues relevant to them at midlife. In order to determine what issues were relevant to middle-aged lesbians, I conducted a pilot study with 21 lesbians between the ages of 40 to 57 (Sang, 1987) who filled out an open-ended questionnaire. The results of this study showed that in contrast to heterosexual midlife women, such concerns as holding a job for the first time, or finding one's identity separate from others, were not relevant to these midlife lesbians.

For this group of mainly professional lesbians, midlife issues were of an existential nature. These lesbian women were concerned with relinquishing past attachments to persons or ideas, refocusing their energies and integrating old and new aspects of the self. Lesbians reported that middle-age was the best time of their lives. They liked themselves better, had more self-confidence and a greater sense of freedom. Because the lesbians in this sample had worked all their lives, midlife was a time to play and have fun. There was less of a need to push as hard as in the past, but paradoxically, their creativity was at its peak. Both relationships and work were an important source of meaning and satisfaction as were the hobbies and interests that each woman was involved in. Each lesbian also appeared to have developed her own life philosophy which gave her life meaning and direction.

In order to determine whether the same results would be obtained with a broader sample of midlife lesbians, I set out to repeat this research with a larger, more diverse group. The data are now being analyzed; however, it appears that the results (so far) are consistent with the pilot study. The main focus of the larger study will once again be on existential issues, but here my focus is restricted to adolescence, career expectations and special interests.

I attributed the creativity and strong sense of self that seemed to characterize lesbians in the pilot study to their having rejected traditional female roles in the course of their development. The purpose of the present study therefore was to explore how middle-aged lesbians saw themselves as adolescents. What were their dreams? Did they have career expectations? Were they non-traditional for adolescents of their time?

SUBJECTS AND METHODOLOGY

The subjects for this study consisted of 110 self-identified lesbians between the ages of 40-59 who completed a midlife lesbian questionnaire. I recruited these women through lesbian newsletters, conferences and organizations. It took over two years to obtain this sample. Each subject filled out a nine page open-ended essay questionnaire which also contained several demographic questions.

The average age of the 110 subjects in this study was 47. Although considerable effort was made to contact minority women, only 5% of this sample were minorities. The subjects are from 24 different states, Canada, Holland and Israel. The states with the highest percentage of subjects were New York (13%) and California (11%). A little more than half (57%) the lesbian women had been married heterosexually at some point in their lives. Forty-four percent of this sample have had one or more children. At the time of the study 67% of the women were in a lesbian relationship of varying duration and the other 33% were single. The lesbians in this study are a highly educated group of women, perhaps even more educated than other lesbian populations that have been studied (Bradford & Ryan, 1987; Daughters of Bilitis, 1958). The majority (78%) of midlife lesbians in this sample were professionals. The others were in business or held working class jobs. About half (52%) held careers or did work that can be considered non-traditional for women, e.g., psychologist, dean, professor, financial analyst and truck driver. Virtually all lesbians in this sample are self-supporting. The average age they became self-supporting was 26 years. In addition to being mostly white and middle-class, this sample is not representative in another respect: 34% are mental health professionals. Considering these biases, the findings may not necessarily apply to all middle-aged lesbians of today.

The subjects were divided into three groups based on the age they considered themselves to be a ''lesbian.'' It was hypothesized that there might be differences in adolescent experiences between women who identified themselves as lesbians in their teens and twenties (Group I, n = 43), women who identified as lesbians in their thirties (Group II, n = 32), and women who identified as lesbians in midlife (Group III, n = 28). The "coming out" age of seven lesbians was unknown.

SUMMARY OF RESULTS AND DISCUSSION

Approximately half the midlife lesbians in this study reported themselves to be non-traditional as adolescents. They described themselves as bookish, rebellious and/or "tomboys" and reported life dreams of career and adventure. The concept of the "life dream" comes from Daniel Levinson's (1978) study of adult male development. The dream is a vague sense of self in an adult world.

The subjects' life dreams in this study were found to fall into three categories: *Traditional Life Dreams* (marriage and family only or no life dreams). *Example*: "I would get married and live the American dream. I don't recall that I had specific dreams of what I wanted to be"; *Traditional and Non-Traditional Life Dreams* (career plus family). *Example*: "A writer who was financially successful. A woman married to a wealthy man with beautiful children"; *Non-Traditional Life Dreams* (career, work, travel, adventure, impact on the world—no mention of marriage and family). *Example*: "I wanted to be independent, professionally successful, in control of my life."

Women who identified as lesbians in their teens and twenties (Group I) were more likely to have had non-traditional life dreams in adolescence (67%), i.e., careers—no marriage, as compared to women who identified as lesbians in their thirties (Group II) or in midlife (Group III). Women who identified themselves as lesbians later in life (Groups II and III) had life dreams that were equally divided between all three life dream categories. In other studies of midlife, women were found to formulate life dreams in their teens and twenties consisting of an image of themselves as wife and as supporter of husbands' goals. Few women reported dreams in which occupation stood as the primary component (Roberts & Newton, 1987; Rubin, 1979).

In order to determine whether more midlife lesbians might report having had career expectations if specifically asked about careers, I included a separate question on career expectations in the questionnaire. The percentage of subjects in the sample who reported career expectations was found to increase slightly (62%). Once again it was found that women who identified as lesbians in their teens and twenties (Group I) were more likely to have had career expectations at an earlier age (79%) as compared to women who identified as lesbians at a later age (Group II, 59% and Group III, 44%). A larger percentage (78%) of the lesbians in Group I who never married were more likely to have had career goals. This would make sense considering that these women did not expect to be taken care of in a traditional marriage and therefore needed some way of providing for themselves economically.

Of the women who did have career aspirations, a little more than half (64%) were of a non-traditional nature, e.g., scientist, doctor, professor, business owner and athlete. The majority of women who came out in their teens and twenties (Group I, 76%) and in their thirties (Group II, 72%) envisioned themselves in non-traditional careers. In contrast, a little less than half (44%) the women who identified themselves as lesbians in midlife expected to be in non-traditional careers. Subjects in this group thought in terms of careers in nursing and teaching.

It is significant to note that although just a little more than half the lesbians in this sample expected to have careers as adults, practically all have careers at the present time. It is mainly the women who identified as lesbians in their teens and twenties (Group I) who showed much less of a discrepancy between their career expectations when younger and their occupational status now. In addition to deriving considerable satisfaction from career and work, lesbians in this sample were found to have many diverse hobbies and interests which also gave their life satisfaction and meaning.

SOME CONCLUDING REMARKS

Part of the working-through process that goes on in midlife appears to be a re-connecting with adolescence, a period in life where many paths and options are open. Levinson (1978) has observed that developmental issues of adolescence are reactivated during the "Midlife Transition." Based on the results of the present study, many midlife lesbians were found to have had a variety of interests and several career possibilities as adolescents. In the pilot study it was found that tapping into this period can result in re-establishing connections with part of the self that had been eliminated in the course of development. A passion for music long since forgotten may be revived with a new sense of pleasure, or those "tomboy" activities may have turned into an interest in the outdoors which is part of a broader life philosophy. Thus, it would appear that the life dreams and special interests that one has as an adolescent can lay the foundation for meaning and satisfaction in later years.

Although adolescence is a time of confusion and uncertainty, it is also a time of vitality and dreams. With the experience that comes with age, combined with the qualities of adolescence, midlife can be a period of heightened creativity. It can be a time of integration or a time to see things in new ways. Based on the subjects' responses to the questionnaire as a whole, midlife lesbians were found to be a creative group of women. Their creativity was expressed in writing, artistic endeavors, spirituality, politics and the development of community.

There is not much known about women's developmental issues at midlife, particularly women who have utilized their potential. It is hoped that this study will help to further our understanding of female development. Existing models of adult development have not taken into account women who, from an early age, did not accept the traditional female role. These women seem to have some different issues at midlife.

REFERENCES

Bradford, J. and Ryan, C. (1987). *The national lesbians health care survey*. Washington, D.C.: National Lesbian and Gay Health Foundation.

Daughters of Bilitis. (1958). Daughters of Bilitis questionnaire reveals some facts about lesbians. *The Ladder,* 9, 1-46, New York: Arno Press.

Junge, M. and Maya, V. (1985). Women in their forties: A group portrait and implications for psychotherapy. *Women and Therapy*, 4, 3-19.

Levinson, D. J. (1978). *The seasons of a man's life*. New York: Ballantine Books.

Lopata, H. and Barnewolt, D. (1984). The middle years: Changes and variations in social-role commitments. In Baruch, G. and Brooks-Gunn, J. (Eds.), *Women in midlife* (pp. 83-108). New York: Plenum Press.

Roberts, P. and Newton, P. M. (1987). Levinsonian studies of women's adult development. *Psychology and Aging*, 2, 154-163.

Rubin, L. B. (1979). *Women of a certain age*. New York: Harper & Row.

Sang, B. E. (1987). *Some existential issues of middle-aged lesbians*. Paper presented at the meeting of the American Psychological Association, Atlanta, GA.

Women in Dual-Career Families and the Challenge of Retirement

Joy B. Reeves, PhD

SUMMARY. The author reviews structural sources of strain that younger dual-career families are likely to experience as first identified by the Rapoports, and extends the analysis to families whose members are about to retire or are retired. The analysis is limited to heterosexual married couples with or without children in a dual-career family. Objectives of this essay are twofold: (1) to lay the groundwork for a theoretically informed empirical study of mature dual-career families and (2) to identify needed areas of research on aging spouses, especially women, in dual-career families.

One of the most significant social movements of recent times is the movement of women into the work force. More women work outside of the home than ever before, and a large proportion (66% between the ages 18 and 44 years) are mothers (U.S. Department of Labor, 1985). As a result of occupational demand, the women's movement, and a more favorable ideological climate for women working outside of the home, women in the professions now outnumber men in the professions as defined by the U.S. Census Bureau (Andersen, 1988; p. 117). Since professional women tend to marry men in high-prestige occupations, the number of dual-career

Joy B. Reeves is Professor of Sociology and Chairman of the Department of Sociology at Stephen F. Austin State University, Nacogdoches, TX. Dr. Reeves received her PhD from Louisiana State University in 1972. Her research interests include sociology of gender roles, sociology of leisure and sociology of work. She has work published in *Journal of Leisure Research, Leisure Sciences, Sociological Spectrum, Deviant Behavior, Sociology of Sport Journal, Sociological Inquiry, Teaching Sociology, Free Inquiry in Sociology, Journal of Pastoral Counseling, Journal of Pastoral Care, Pastoral Psychology, The Texas Journal of Science, The Humanist Sociologist* and other journals.

families is expected to increase (Pepitone-Rockwell, 1980). In this essay, dual-career family is defined as a type of family form in which married heterosexual couples with or without children pursue active family lives and full-time work careers rather than jobs. (A job is a typically salaried position with limited future mobility; a career usually requires more education and consists of steps leading to advancement within that career.) Researchers expect an upsurge in the growth of dual-career families approaching retirement age near the end of this century (Davidson, 1982).

Even though dual-career families are expected to increase in the future, very few researchers have studied mature dual-career families, the exceptions being Wartenberg and Ulbrich (1986), Anderson et al., (1980) and Jewson (1982). Here, I review the structural sources of strain younger dual-career families are likely to experience and then extend the analysis to older families whose members are about to retire or are retired. I hope to lay the groundwork for a theoretically informed empirical study of mature dual-career families, and identify needed areas of research on such families, with particular emphasis on older women.

REVIEW OF LITERATURE

I reviewed the literature on dual-career families and mature married professional women about to retire or who have already retired who may or may or may not be in dual-career families. All researchers agree that dual-career families are stress-producing, but there is no clear cut agreement by researchers on whether joining two careers in one family leads to a substantial change in family form or gender roles as a result of stress. The Rapoports (1971) claim the structure of dual-career families has the potential for producing greater gender equality. This position is espoused by Dizard (1968), Garland (1972), Miller (1972), Bailyn (1970) and Hertz (1986). Others say the dual career family structure does not necessarily change to one that is more egalitarian (Weingarten, 1978; Bird, 1979; Holmstrom, 1973; Keating & Cole, 1980; Kerchoff, 1966; Szinovacz, 1982). Knowledge about the extent of family structure and gender role change may be important in predicting successful adjustment to retirement by spouses, especially women, in dual-career families.

In an exploratory study of retired dual-career spouses, Wartenberg and Ulbrich (1981) found life satisfaction, as well as power and decision-making, are related to couple relationships prior to the husband's retirement. Wife's life satisfaction was also related to length of husband's retirement, perception of husband's attitudes toward her employment, and recent thoughts of divorce. While retired husbands tend to help more with household tasks, the wife continues to bear the responsibility for them, which conforms to the findings of younger spouses in dual-career families (Jewson, 1982). In a study that controlled for type of family, women in mature dual-career families were more likely than women in traditional families to have earned a private pension benefit and have social security benefits that exceeded the benefits to spouse of workers (Anderson et al., 1980). Retirement may be a welcome, satisfying change for women in dual-career families because they experience decreasing mobility at work as they age (Roberts, 1984), achieve less than their spouses professionally (Bryson & Bryson, 1980; Yogev, 1981), and experience sex discrimination at work (Benokratis & Feagin, 1986).

Not much exists in the literature on the subject of retired married professional women. Szinovacz (1982) produced the best compilation of the literature on this subject. In general, research shows work is meaningful to professional women (Atchley, 1976; Jacobson, 1974), retirement often does create a dilemma for women (Jewson, 1982; Foner & Schwab, 1981), and women are not often well rehearsed for retirement (Bock, 1984; Davidson, 1982; Behling et al., 1983). Retirement constitutes a crisis for many women in low-paying occupations who are single, divorced, widowed or have husbands who did not adequately prepare for retirement in a financial sense. Only 67% of women aged 55 to 64 are married; the percentage drops to 47% between the ages of 65 and 74 years. Approximately 82% of men aged 55 to 74 years are married (Bock, 1984). Price-Bonham and Johnson (1982) reported that only 29% of married professional women in their sample had paid into any re-

tirement fund of their own and that 50% of them opted not to participate in a retirement program. In general, professional women compared to men are less prepared for retirement (Behling et al., 1983).

The research is mixed as to whether or not professional women,
compared to various populations such as men or non-professional
women, look forward to retirement and make a positive adjustment.
Some do (Cavaghan, 1981; Holahan, 1981; Foner & Schwab, 1981;
Rosen & Palmer, 1981; Atchley, 1976; Campbell, 1979), and some
do not (Price-Bonham & Johnson, 1982; Simpson et al., 1966).
Positive retirement adjustment is significantly related to positive
pre-retirement attitudes, a positive self-concept (Rosen & Palmer,
1982), and the orderliness or continuity of one's career (Simpson et
al., 1966). When these factors are absent, retirement may not be a
satisfying experience.

The lack of consistency in pre-retirement attitudes and retirement
satisfaction research calls for resolution. Few of the studies controlled for type of family form (dual-career vs. traditional; egalitarian vs. traditional), gender identity of both spouses, and whether or
not the spouses were in a female or male-dominated profession/
occupation. These variables and how they interact with each other
need to be considered in future retirement studies. More than likely
some of the research inconsistencies arise from using nonrepresen-
tative, specialized samples (nuns; academics; self-employed; social
workers; education specialists), noncomparable units of analysis,
and different data collection methods.

THEORETICAL FRAMEWORK AND ANALYSIS

From a family system perspective (Riley, 1983; Nye, 1976), the
family is a system of interdependent roles. The social relationships
among family members are never fixed, but change as the family
members grow older, and as society, itself, changes. Family and
work systems are interrelated; for most of us, renegotiation of work/
family balance continues throughout work life. Renegotiation is intensified at times of transition, such as when a baby is born, the
children leave home, or a spouse retires. Important role changes
influence the family decision-making process, and the choices
made at these points of transition will determine a new phase in the

dual-career family, and with it a new pattern of stress (Bebbington, 1973).

A complex interrelationship exists among ideology, social structure, and behavior. When ideology, social structure and behavior are inconsistent, structural stress is produced and strain is experienced by individuals. Sometimes the strain is so great that social changes occur. A dual-career family is a relatively new type of family form whose members are subject to various strains because cultural patterns that permit adaptation at various stages of dual-career family life have not yet crystallized (Hunt & Hunt, 1982). Few middle-age spouses in dual-career families know what to expect in retirement because few older spouses have had experience with this type of family form. The Rapoports (1971), who expanded on the works of Goode (1960) and Wilensky (1962), identified five sources of structural stress in dual-career families: role overload, social network dilemmas, normative dilemmas, maintenance of personal identity, and role-cycling. I will review the Rapoports' analysis and extend it to mature dual-career spouses about to retire or already retired.

ROLE OVERLOAD
AND SOCIAL NETWORK DILEMMAS

In dual-career families both spouses belong to a number of groups and therefore perform multiple roles. The necessity of the husband and wife to perform adequately all of the tasks in the domestic environment as well as their employment careers often results in role overload and social network dilemmas. Costs and strains are largely borne by women in dual-career families; where husbands are not supportive, the whole arrangement is exceedingly fragile (Johnson & Johnson, 1980). Perhaps this is why there is a higher divorce rate for dual-career spouses than for traditional spouses (Nadelson & Nadelson, 1980) or why in the recent past successful career women tended to be childless, divorced, or single (Astin, 1969; Hunt & Hunt, 1982).

According to the Rapoports (1971), dual-career families cope with this stress by curtailing nonessential social activities and leisure, especially on the part of the wife. When spouses limit social activities this tends to weaken their social networks and leaves the spouses more vulnerable in times of crisis. If these spouses, especially wives, restrict the size of their social circle and curtail their leisure in their younger married years, what kind of adjustment can we expect from these spouses in their retirement years when social networks and leisure are supposed to assume greater importance? Do spouses committed to a work ethic for twenty years just pick up a leisure lifestyle when they have had little or no experience with leisure? People have to learn to value leisure just as they have to learn to value work; however, our culture, with its work ethic legacy, makes it especially difficult for professionals to appreciate leisure. In general, the research indicates people continue their lifestyle from pre-retirement to the retirement period; the aging process does not normally bring about a fundamental change in the type or quality of leisure behavior (Parker, 1983, p.69). Lack of appreciation for and experience with leisure in pre-retirement years may constitute an especially potent source of stress in retirement for professional spouses in dual-career families.

How easy would it be for dual-career spouses to expand their social circle when for years they consciously held it to a minimum? A wide variety of friends can help individuals develop themselves as persons and can keep a marriage potentially interesting if new ideas and experiences derived from friends are shared with the spouse. Would dependence on a small circle of friends for social stimulation over an extended period of time tend to restrict personality expansion, inhibit a person from interacting in new social situations, and make for a less interesting marriage? Since role flexibility is greater in dual-career families than in traditional families, aging dual-career spouses may very well adapt more readily than traditional spouses to changes in their life-cycles and expand their social circles. Continuity and discontinuity in social patterns for couples in various types of family forms over time would seem to be a fruitful area of research.

NORMATIVE DILEMMAS

Normative dilemmas arise through discrepancies in the way people believe they ought to live and the way people actually live, producing stress for dual-career families. Spouses in dual-career families ideally support egalitarian relationships between spouses, but the society offers little support for such a relationship. This is why women, by and large, continue to follow their traditional priorities of fitting their employment schedules to their family responsibilities, rather than the reverse, as men do (Degler, 1980, p.436). Hertz (1986), who studied only affluent dual-career spouses in corporate work settings, said high incomes were necessary for dual-career marriages to work, since services and goods must be purchased to make possible a more egalitarian lifestyle. The Rapoports (1971), who studied both affluent and nonaffluent dual-career spouses, concluded affluence is not a necessary condition for a workable dual-career family. Longitudinal studies that control for social class are needed to test this thesis more adequately.

Discrepancies between personal beliefs and social norms may be a particular source of stress to the professional wife in a dual-career family because society emphasizes wives' maternal and homemaking role. A husband who takes on domestic roles commits a less intense norm violation than a wife who delegates a large part of the child-rearing role to someone else (Rapoports, 1971). The Rapoports (1971) found spouses in dual-career families cope with this dilemma by selecting other couples who are most like themselves to be their friends. Dual-career spouses also tend to compartmentalize or segment their various roles to reduce the strain they experience in their lives. For example, women attempt to leave their family problems at home while they are at work and attempt to leave their work problems at the office when they are home.

Some norm dilemmas would seem to lessen considerably for retired dual-career spouses. For example, it would be unnecessary for retired spouses to insulate themselves from social criticism ("How can you be a good mother and also have a career?") by selecting other dual-career spouses as friends. Mature dual-career spouses can blend in easily with others who did not have a family lifestyle similar to theirs in earlier years. Work may no longer be a basis of identity for either retired spouse and consequently not serve as a criterion for selecting friends. Provided the retired spouses can reactivate rusty interpersonal skills, and more discretionary time is available to them, retirement can be an opportunity for dual-career spouses to expand their social circle.

Other norm dilemmas may continue into retirement. Consider the continuity of women's care-taking/nurturant role. Dual-career women may choose to retire earlier than they had planned because they are expected to care for an elderly parent or other relatives. Hasty retirement may lack planning, and lack of pre-retirement planning negatively affects adjustment in retirement (Bock, 1984).

If dual-career spouses do not retire at the same time, dilemmas become evident in conflicts over household duties. Dual-career spouses must renegotiate their relationship when one spouse retires and repeat the process when the other retires. A spouse used to sharing household duties when he/she worked full-time may very well dislike assuming the full burden of household chores in retirement, yet the spouse who is still working may feel he/she should not have to do any household chores. Jewson's study (1982) of retired spouses in dual-career families indicates retired husbands tend to help more with household tasks, but the wife continues to bear the responsibility for them.

The Rapoports (1971) found parents in dual-career families were concerned with their children; they were not self-centered and anti-children, a sentiment often expressed by parents in traditional families about dual-career parents. Given this concern with children, and the fact that one of the perceived costs to women in this type of family structure is less involvement with children than desired, it is conceivable that as these women enter retirement years their children and grandchildren may become very important in deciding where to locate. If one or both spouses want to continue his/her professional life after retirement, such as write articles for publication or conduct workshops, how important would easy access to work facilities and grandchildren be to one or both members who have officially retired? The potential for conflict between work/family roles would continue to exist for the retired spouses, but its intensity is probably less severe than when they and their children were younger (Witt & Goodale, 1981).

MAINTENANCE OF PERSONAL IDENTITY

The Rapoports (1971) found spouses in dual-career families had problems with identity. Such problems stem from the socio-cultural definition of work as inherently "masculine" while homemaking and family rearing is "feminine." Implied is the idea that cultural confusion of gender role results in psychological or even physical confusion, as reflected in impotence or frigidity (Bebbington, 1973).

Retirement can produce an identity crisis for a married professional woman because she has deliberately chosen to reject the position of full time housewife. Her return to an earlier rejected status may result in considerable strain for both her and her husband. As with professional men, her personal identity may in large part come from work. If both spouses retire concurrently, and both identify with their work, then retirement is likely to produce difficulty for the couple because both would be struggling simultaneously with identity problems. A wife in pain could hardly ease her husband's pain during their mutual transition to retirement or vice-versa. A profitable area of research would be to study personal identities of both spouses in dual-career families and how these may or may not change with various role transitions in the life-cycle.

ROLE-CYCLING DILEMMAS

Spouses in dual-career families experience problems relative to the timing of the demands associated with work and family roles. For example, when children are very young, the demands of the mother role may take priority over the demands of the work role. Spouses must decide the best time periods for one or both partners to assume greater work responsibilities. Role-cycling dilemmas derive from organizational problems at critical stages in the life-cycle as when the dual-career couple decides to start a family or one of the partners decides to accept a more demanding career position. Since careers do not peak for women at the same time they do for men due to discrimination, late entry, delayed parenthood, and adjustment of career needs to family needs, there is a lack of integration of the three social systems (work system of wife; work system of husband; family system). It is this lack of integration that produces the role-cycling dilemmas for dual-career families. To what extent are these dilemmas increased or decreased as spouses in such families age?

As dual-career spouses enter retirement age, role-cycling dilemmas may become ever more problematic than when the spouses were younger. For example, the spouses may experience retirement at different times. Almost one-third of the wives whose husbands retired between the ages of 65 and 69 years had not yet retired (Fox, 1979). This situation increases the role complexity of the spouses. Due to a shorter pre-retirement employment history, married professional women may not be ready to retire when spouses wish to retire. One spouse may retire fully whereas the other may not retire at all or only partially.

Rather than just three social systems to consider in the cycling process, additional ones are added as the spouses age, such as the leisure systems of both husband and wife. Each spouse could have a separate leisure system, and both could share one. The spouse who works part-time or full time may not be available to share some of the leisure pursuits desired by the retired partner, such as frequent travel. Does the retired spouse take trips alone if the other spouse is unable to participate because of work commitments? Out of loneliness, the retired partner may pressure the working spouse to retire. Should a wife who delayed entry into the work world to please her husband also retire early so she can be a better companion to him? What happens to friendship circles of dual-career spouses when one spouse retires early? If dual-career spouses select other dual-career spouses for friends and the status of one partner changes, do the once compatible friends dissolve their friendship?

When spouses do not retire concurrently decisions about where to retire must be postponed. In addition, questions about who adjusts to whose time schedule are likely to occur. Does the retired spouse adjust to the spouse who is working? Even though most women in dual-career families adjust their schedules to fit their husband's schedule (Holmstrom, 1973; Bird, 1979; Weingarten, 1978; Lips, 1988), this may not be the case among mature women in this type of family. In the interest of equity these women may very well expect a shift on the part of their husbands (Bailyn, 1970).

Mature spouses in dual-career families may redefine their roles and possibly reexamine what retirement should be. Is retirement a time to be together with the spouse, a time to be less responsible to others, or a time to be more responsible to others? To what extent aging dual-career spouses hold compatible views on retirement should be researched.

Concurrent retirement of spouses in dual-career families may be less problematic than sequential retirement. And, because of this, it may be more common. A wife's attachment to the work force significantly raises the probability of her husband deferring retirement (Davidson, 1982; Anderson et al., 1980), and this may also increase the probability of concurrent retirement. Other factors that increase the probability of concurrent retirement are age of spouse, high economic status and amount of pension coverage (Henretta & O'Rand, 1983). Research indicates that dual-career spouses retire later than those who are not (Anderson et al., 1980), but we do not know why this is the case. An interesting area to explore would be the consequences of career couples following different retirement patterns.

CONCLUSION

The dual-career family form is stress-producing, but the nature and extent of stress may vary depending on the life-cycle of the partners involved. If our society becomes less stratified by sex, it will be easier to make a dual-career family work and this will encourage couples who "want to have it all" to consider adopting this type of family form. Whether or not this type of family form works well in the late years of life is largely unknown because too few spouses in dual-career families have reached this stage and of those who have, we know little about them. We need to pursue the neglected study of aging spouses in dual-career families to answer the many questions discussed here. In so doing we will contribute to the development of leisure, retirement, gender role, family, and gerontology theory, as well as facilitate the work of practitioners who develop programs for the aged, who are disproportionately women, and therapists, who counsel married couples contemplating marriage or divorce.

REFERENCES

Andersen, M. (1988). *Thinking about women.* New York: Macmillan.
Anderson, K., Clark R., and Johnson, T. (1980). "Retirement in dual-career families." In R. Clark (Ed.), *Retirement policy in an aging society* (pp. 109-127) Durham, NC: Duke University Press.
Astin, H. (1969). *The woman doctorate in America.* New York: Russell Sage.
Atchley, R. (1976). Adjustment to loss of job at retirement. *International Journal of Aging and Human Development 31*:204-211.

Bailyn, L. (1970). Career and family orientation of husbands and wives in relation to mental happiness. *Human Relations 22*:97-113.

Bebbington, A.C. (1973). The function of stress in the establishment of the dual-career family. *Journal of Marriage and the Family 35*:530-537.

Behling, J., Kilty, K., and Foster, S. (1983). Scarce resources for retirement planning: A dilemma for professional women. *Journal of Gerontological Social Work 5*:49-60.

Benokratis, N., and Feagin, J. (1986). *Modern sexism*. New York: Prentice-Hall.

Bird, C. (1979). *The two-paycheck marriage*. New York: Pocket Books.

Bock, M. (1984). Retirement preparation needs of women. In H. Dennis (Ed.), *Retirement preparation* (pp. 129-140). Lexington, KY: Lexington Books.

Bryson, R., and Bryson, J. (1980). Salary and job performance difference in dual-career couples. In F. Pepitone-Rockwell (Ed.), *Dual-career couples* (pp. 241-259). London: Sage.

Campbell, S. (1979). Delayed mandatory retirement and the working women. *The Gerontologist 19*:257-263.

Cavaghan, P. (1981). *Social adjustment of women to retirement.* Unpublished doctoral dissertation, University of California, Davis.

Davidson, J. (1982). Issues of employment and retirement in the lives of women over age 40. In N. Osgood (Ed.), *Life after work* (pp. 95-114). New York: Praeger.

Degler, C. (1980). *At odds: Women and the family in America from the revolution to the present.* New York: Oxford University Press.

Dizard, J. (1968). *Social change in the family.* Chicago: University of Chicago Press.

Foner, A., and Schwab, K. (1981). *Aging and retirement.* Monterey, CA: Brooks/Cole.

Fox, J. (1979). Earnings replacement notes of retired couples: Findings from the retirement history study. *Social Security Bulletin 42*:17-39.

Garland, T. (1972). The better half: The male in the dual-career professional family. In C. Safilios-Rothschild (Ed.), *Toward a sociology of women* (pp. 199-216). Lexington, MA: Xerox College Publishing.

Goode, W. (1960). A theory of role strain. *American Sociological Review 25*: 483-496.

Henretta, John C., and O'Rand, A. (1983). Joint retirement in the dual worker family. *Social Forces 62*:504-520.

Hertz, R. (1986). *More equal than others: Women and men in dual-career marriages*. Berkeley: University of California Press.

Holmstrom, L. (1973). *The two-career family.* Cambridge, MA: Schenkman.

Holohan, C. (1981). Lifetime achievement patterns, retirement and life satisfaction of gifted aged women. *Journal of Gerontology 36*:741-749.

Hunt, J., and Hunt, L. (1982). The dualities of careers and families: New integration or new polarizations? *Social Problems 29*:499-510.

Jacobson, C. (1974). Rejection of the retiree role: A study of female industrial workers in their 50's. *Human Relations 27*:477-492.

Jewson, R. (1982). After retirement: An exploratory study of the professional woman. In M. Szinovacz (Ed.), *Women's retirement* (pp. 169-194). Beverly Hills: Sage.

Johnson, C., and Johnson, F. (1980). Parenthood, marriage and careers: Situational constraints and role strain. In F. Pepitone-Rockwell (Ed.), *Dual-career couples* (pp. 143-161). London: Sage.

Keating N., and Cole, P. (1980). What do I do with him 24 hours a day? Change in the housewife role after retirement. *The Gerontologist 20*:84-89.

Kerchoff, D. (1966). Family pattern and morale in retirement. In I. Simpson and J. McKinney (Ed.), *Social aspects of aging* (pp. 172-194). Durham, NC: Duke University Press.

Lipps, H. (1988). *Sex and gender*. Mountain View, CA: Mayfield.

Miller, S. (1972). The making of a confused middle-aged husband. In C. Safilios-Rothschild (Ed.), *Toward sociology of women* (pp. 245-254). Lexington, MA: Xerox College Publishing.

Nadelson, C., and Nadelson, T. (1980). Dual-career marriages: benefits and costs. In F. Pepitone-Rockwell (Ed.), *Dual-career couples* (pp. 91-109). London: Sage.

Nye, F.I. (1976). *Role structure: An analysis of the family*. Beverly Hills: Sage.

Parker, S. (1983). *Leisure and work*. London: Allen and Unwin.

Pepitone-Rockwell, F. (Ed.) (1980). *Dual-career couples*. London: Sage.

Price-Bonham S., and Johnson, C. (1982). Attitudes toward retirement: A comparison of professional and nonprofessional married women. In M. Szinovacz (Ed.), *Women's retirement* (pp. 123-138). Beverly Hills: Sage.

Rapoport, R., and Rapoport, R. (1971). *Dual-career families*. Harmondsworth, England: Penguin Books.

Riley, M. (1983). The family in an aging society: A matrix of latent relationships. *Journal of Family Issues 4*:439-454.

Roberts, C. (1984). The role of employment in women's lives: Some findings from a British survey of women and employment. *Sociologie du Travail 26*:317-325.

Rosen, J., and Palmer, M. (1982). Retirement adaptations and self-concepts in professional women. Paper presented at the annual convention of the American Psychological Assoc., Washington, DC (Aug 23-27).

Simpson, I., Back, K., and McKinney, J. (1966). Orientation toward work and retirement. In I. Simpson and J. McKinney (Eds.), *Social aspects of aging* (pp. 45-54). Durham, NC: Duke University Press.

Szinovacz, M. (Ed.) (1982). *Women's retirement*. Beverly Hills: Sage.

U.S. Department of Labor (1985). *Employment and earnings* (Vol. 34). Washington, DC: U.S. Government Printing Office.

Wartenberg, H., and Ulbrich, P. (1986). Women's timing of retirement and life satisfaction in dual-career families. Paper presented to International Sociological Association. U. of Miami. Coral Gables, FL.

Weingarten, K. (1978). The employment pattern of professional couples and their distribution of involvement in the family. *Psychology of Women Quarterly* 3:43-53.

Wilkinsky, H. (1962). Life cycle, mark situations and social participation. In C. Tibbets and W. Donahue (Eds.), *Social aspects of aging* (pp. 40-56). New York: Columbia University Press.

Witt, P., and Goodale, T. (1981). The relationship between farmers to leisure enjoyment and family stages. *Leisure Sciences* 4:29-49.

Yogev, S. (1981). Do professional women have egalitarian marital relationships? *Journal of Marriage and the Family* 43:865-871.

Invention Begins at Forty:
Older Women of the 19th Century
as Inventors

Autumn Stanley

SUMMARY. This paper examines a group of prolific women inventors, all specializing in machines, and all arguably professional inventors for some or all of their working lives. The group is interesting in its very existence, which contradicts time-honored stereotypes against woman as inventors, and especially as professional inventors. However, it is particularly interesting for its high average age at first patent and its continuation of patent and/or inventive activity into old age. Data on the women's marital and economic status and social class are presented where available, and the group is compared with a sample of nonprofessional women inventors who exhibited at the Philadelphia Centennial of 1876.

One of the largest gaps in scholarship — and thinking — on women and aging is the achievement perspective. Even with the new interest in "senior citizens" driven by the graying of the American market,[1] our elders, particularly older women, are still more often seen as victims or "problems" than as valuable contributors to society. It is this gap that I wish to address here, focusing on contributions to technology.

Initially, I intended simply to present examples of women who either started inventing late or kept on inventing into their 60s and

---

Autumn Stanley completed much of this research while she was Affiliated Scholar with the Institute for Research on Women and Gender at Stanford University. The author wishes to express her gratitude to several members of the Institute, as well as the Institute for Historical Study, for emotional support and intellectual stimulation.

Correspondence regarding this article should be addressed to Autumn Stanley, 241 Bonita, Los Trancos Woods, Portola Valley, CA 94025.

---

[1]Consumers over fifty will soon be more numerous — and already have more money — than the teenagers and young adults American advertisers and marketers have recently targeted.

70s, and let the group speak for itself.[2] Women today can expect long lives, and we need more models who, like Imogen Cunningham and Georgia O'Keefe, continue to create not only past 45 or 65, but even past 90. So little is known about women inventors that such a compilation seemed valuable in itself.

However, as I worked, something more interesting began to emerge: the idea that **the older woman inventor might be the rule rather than the exception,** or at least far more common than I would have predicted.

Popular wisdom locates creativity in youth—the late teens and early 20s. Later work may be solid, but will lack that early fire. Without reviewing the recent literature on creativity, I wish to point out a few things relevant to our discussion here: First, most of what has been written on age and creativity focuses on males and male career paths. Second, the age of greatest creativity varies with the field of endeavor. Third, invention involves not just the initial creative idea, but its practical realization. Here, such factors as patience, determination, self-confidence, available technology—and money—enter in. It is one thing, as Charles Babbage and Ada Lovelace learned to their sorrow, to conceive of a computer, and quite another to build it.

Inventors can be classified in various ways, according to output, specialization (or lack thereof), technological significance, whether they are employed or independent, and whether they are professional inventors or invent upon occasion, for money, fun or some necessity in their other work—among others.

Age may relate to invention in different ways in these various groups, and between women and men. Moreover, a woman's place in her life cycle and her level of family commitments may be more pertinent than age *per se,* though the two are often related. To take the most obvious example, a woman of 25 with three small children at home seems less likely to patent an invention than another woman of 25 who has no such commitments. Likewise, a woman of 45 who cares for her invalid mother, as opposed to her same-age

---

[2]Earlier versions of this paper were presented to the Western Association of Women Historians in Davis, California, in May 1987, and to the National Women's Studies Association convention in Atlanta, Georgia, in June of that year.

cousin whose parents are dead. Ideally, therefore, in addition to such "male" career-determining variables as education, training, mentors, and career stage, a proper study of women inventors should look at marital and child-rearing status, responsibility for aged relatives, and other life-cycle variables. Economic factors are also pertinent, and we should look at social class and family finances.[3] Unfortunately, this information is not available for many 19th century women inventors, virtually all of whom are excluded from all the standard biographical sources.[4]

Supposing for the moment that a crucial division is that between professional and occasional inventors, let us look at two 19th-century samples of women inventors, one professional or quasi-professional and the other almost entirely occasional, to see what they can tell us about age-related patterns of female inventive creativity.

PROFESSIONAL SAMPLE

These are 14 women identified during research for my book (Stanley, 1990), who by self-definition, peer-definition, span of patent/invention dates, nature, number, and significance of inventions, income from inventions, or some combination of these criteria, can arguably be called professional inventors. Though some of them lived and worked into the 20th century, all are basically 19th-century figures.

All of these women specialized in machines or mechanical de-

---

[3]The effects of the latter can be paradoxical. That is, an inventive woman may invent and patent her inventions because wealth enables her to do so — or because she is forced to do something to make money. The relationship between these two opposing influences and age, if any, is unclear, though I suspect that the more extreme forms of both the enabling and the forcing economic factors would be somewhat more likely to occur later rather than earlier in a woman's life.

[4]The first-series index volume to the *Dictionary of American Biography* lists only one woman as an inventor: Amanda T. Jones. *Notable American Women* classes only three women as inventors (Jones, Margaret Knight, and Sybilla Masters) in its first edition (James, James, & Boyer, 1971: hereinafter, *NAW*/1), and none at all in its second (Sicherman & Green, 1980; hereinafter, *NAW*/2). Furthermore, *NAW* sometimes omits the inventions of profiled women, e.g., Jane Swisshelm and Lillian Russell. Marital and socioeconomic data presented here have been dug out of primary sources (see f.n. 6).

vices; that is, more than half of their patents or known inventions were mechanical in nature. I drew my sample this way deliberately in order to make it more nearly comparable with the male inventor stereotype,[5] but it also turns out that *most of the most prolific female inventors* (as judged by patents held) *specialized in mechanical invention* (see Table 1).

None of these women is well known now, though **Helen Blanchard** and **Mary Carpenter** to a limited degree, and **Knight, Jones,** and **Hosmer** to a greater degree, were nationally known in their day. Hosmer was a famous sculptor: Jones, a well-known writer and spiritualist; Blanchard, a socially prominent entrepreneur and philanthropist (*NAW*/1; Willard & Livermore, 1893). Since their patents are the most noteworthy thing about most of these women, let us look at this patent output, keeping in mind that they may have *invented* many other things as well.

Eliza Alexander: Six sewing-machine patents, and a Lawn-tennis apparatus.[6] Interestingly, Alexander's first (1857) and second (1873) patents are separated by 16 years (LWP).[7] The famous journalist and historian Ida Tarbell considered her a professional inventor (1887: 357), making her the first example of the "Many women [who] have made a business of inventing and putting their goods on the market." I have no personal or financial data on Alexander, but

---

[5]In other words, my original selection of this group had nothing to do with age as a variable. The women were discovered in the course of lengthy research on women inventors, the results of which are soon to be published as *Mothers of Invention: Notes for a Revised History of Technology* (1989). Biographical information comes from census records, city directories, contemporary newspapers and periodicals, and, rarely, from contemporary biographical dictionaries and *NAW* (see text below for details).

[6]By convention I will capitalize the first word of a formal patent description of an invention, to signal that this is Patent Office wording. The lawn tennis apparatus is a pronged attachment for the end of a tennis racquet, enabling a player to retrieve balls from unreachable spots, or pick up balls without bending over. This patent is omitted by the only known list of 19th-century women patentees (U.S. Patent Office, 1888-95: hereinafter, LWP).

[7]Patent data come from LWP or, if omitted from LWP or if more detailed information was needed, from official patent records (patents themselves, annual name lists of patentees, and weekly patent gazettes).

TABLE 1

FOURTEEN 19th-C. U.S. PROFESSIONAL WOMEN INVENTORS
(Specializing in Machines)

U = Unknown   P = Patents.   I = Unpatented Inventions   T = Total

Name	Patenting span	Residence	P	I	T+
Eliza Alexander	(1857-82)	NYC	7	U	7
Maria Beasley (1847-?1904)	(1878-98)	Philadelphia, Chicago	15	U	15
Mildred Blakey	(1874-1904)	var. PA cities*	14	U	14
Helen Blanchard (1840-1922)	(1873-1914)	Portland, ME; Boston, Phila., NYC	28	U	28
Mary Carpenter	(1862-94)	Buffalo, SF, NYC	13**	U	13
Ella Gaillard	(1874-92)	SF, NYC	8	U	8
Harriet Hosmer (1830-1908)	(1878-81)	Watertown, MA; Italy, London	5++	2(U)	7
Amanda Jones (1835-1914)	(1873-1914)	Clinton, WI; Chicago; Junct. City, KS; Brooklyn	12	2(U)	14
Margaret Knight (1838-1914)	(1871-1912)	Framingham, Boston, MA	24	c65	c89
Bertha Lammé (1869-1943)	(1893-1905)	Pittsburgh, PA	0	U#	U
Mary J. Montgomery	(1860s)	NYC	3	U	3
Mary S. (c.1851-80)	(c1870-80)	St. Louis, MO	53*+	U	53
Emily E. Tassey (1823-99)	(1876-80)	McKeesport, Pittsburgh, PA	5	U	5
Harriet Tracy	(1868-93)	NYC, New Brighton, NY	16	1##	17

+ This figure is an absolute minimum. Usually I know only number of patents held; even where I know of unpatented inventions, I do not know how many. Knight's total comes from an interview done in her old age, and may be a low estimate.

* Blakey lived in Etna, Alleghany, Hazelwood, and Pittsburgh, PA, and in Rome, OH, according to patent addresses.

** Not counting her several reissue patents.

++ Hosmer patented her synthetic marble (US), and applied for 4 British patents for magnetic motors (one finalized). She may have patented her mechanical page-turning device for musicians. Her new modeling technique in sculpture was unpatented. Her total known inventions number at least 7. Hosmer was a child inventor, and worked on magnetic motors/perpetual motion until her death in 1908. If she started at age 10, her inventive span (as opposed to her patenting span) is 68 years!

Lammé held no patents in her own name, but worked on a corporate innovation team (Westinghouse) for 12 years; the num-number of important motors and generators she helped design could arguably equal the hundreds patented by her brother Benjamin and other teammates during those years.

#+ Mary S. held no patents in her own name, but sold 53 inventions to agents who patented them (Smith, Apr. 1891, p. 2).

One of Tracy's elevator inventions may have been patented by someone else.

Tarbell presumably used her as an example of an inventor-entrepreneur because she was successful.

In fact, it might be a reasonable assumption that getting a patent in the 19th century required a middle class income, for the application and filing fees alone ($35 from the mid-1870s through the century) would be ten weeks' wages for the poorer working women. With fees for a patent attorney[8] and a model-maker, a patent could easily cost $100 (Warner, 1979, p. 105), eight months' wages for many women.

Maria Beasley (1847-c.1904): Fifteen patents, nine of which were for machines or mechanical devices. Six of the 9 dealt with barrel-making, and at least one was extremely profitable. Beasley's barrel-hooping machine alone reportedly brought her $20,000 per year (Logan, 1912, p. 885). She may have been a manufacturer and entrepreneur as well as an inventor, for Charlotte Smith[9] says that Mrs. Beasley turns out hundreds of ready-made barrels in a day, and oil and sugar refiners pay her profitable royalties from her inventions (Apr. 1891: [4]). She also patented an apparatus for preventing train derailments (1898).

In the Chicago directory she listed her occupation as "Inventor" (1891-6). Thus, both she herself and two contemporary sources counted her a professional inventor. Whatever class she was born into (Presbyterian church affiliation and marriage to a "mechanic" are indications), $20,000 a year in pre-income-tax days was a great fortune.

Mildred Blakey: Fourteen patents, most pertaining to the manufacture of metal pipe and tubing. Examples are a Machine for welding and finishing pipes (1875); a Machine for forming hollow welded cylinders (1876); and a Machine for corrugating pipe sockets (1877). In the late 1890s Blakey patented a Gas or other explo-

---

[8]Only one of the women showing inventions in the Women's Pavilion at the Philadelphia Centennial in 1876 handled her first patent without an attorney. About 75% of the 79 exhibited inventions were patented (1979, pp. 105, 109).

[9]Charlotte Smith (1843-1917) was a magazine editor and publisher, labor leader, reformer, and advocate for women's economic rights from the late 1870s until her death. She was particularly concerned with women inventors, and published a short-lived periodical called the *Woman Inventor*.

sive engine (1897) and a method for the Operation of gas engines (1896). Blakey patented fairly regularly throughout the 35 years of her known inventive career, with five years the longest interval between patents.

Helen Augusta Blanchard: Twenty-eight patents, making her one of the two or three most prolific female patentees of the century. Most noteworthy are her 12 sewing machine patents, since they include zigzag sewing and the machine to do it: five listed simply as Sewing machines; four Hat-sewing machines, one Overseaming machine, one Crochet attachment, and one for Selvage sewing. Her Sewing machine needles (three patents) and her patent pertaining to Making split needles pertain to parts of sewing machines, and her Pencil-sharpener of 1884 is definitely mechanical.

Between 1873, the year of her first patent, at age 33, and 1901, when she was over 60, Helen Blanchard patented regularly, often an invention a year. After 1901 her patent activity slowed. Six years elapsed between her next two patents, and seven between the next pair. But she never stopped patenting altogether until the year before her disabling stroke of 1916. At her last patent (1915) she was 75.

Oldest child of a wealthy shipping merchant in Portland, ME, and distantly related to the famous American inventor Thomas Blanchard (1788-1864), she never married, living with a sister until the sister died, and then with a niece. Her family background and her acquired wealth make her upper class, and a contemporary biographical dictionary agrees (Willard & Livermore, 1893).[10]

Mary P. Carpenter: Thirteen patents (plus reissues). Eight of the thirteen were machines or mechanical in nature: five pertaining to sewing machines; an Ironing and fluting machine; an Improved mop-wringer, and a Barrel-painting machine. One of her sewing-machine inventions, a Needle-and-arm improvement with an exceptionally easy threading needle, was important enough to be men-

---

[10]Other information on Helen and her family and on Blanchard genealogy comes from Arthur Gerrier, Maine Historical Society; Joan Hayden, genealogist, Yarmouth, Maine; Carolyn Cooper, History of Science Department, Yale University; and Pat Curry of Richmond, California.

tioned in a *Scientific American* article of 1870 ("Carpenter Self-Threading . . .," Sept. 10, p. 164), and Carpenter exhibited a sewing machine at the Philadelphia Centennial (Warner, 1979, pp. 111-12). Her five other inventions were a Button, a Grated shovel, a Device for numbering houses, a Netting canopy for beds, and a Mosquito trap. Her patent dates, spanning more than 30 years, show an interesting nine-year hiatus between 1876 and 1885.

Ella N. Gaillard: Eight patents, four of them unmistakably mechanical: a Musical top (1876), a "Fountain" (a combined portable spring powered fountain and music box; 1885), a Musical watch (1886), and a Combined paperweight, calendar, and musical watch (1889). If she was wife, sister, or daughter to the shoemaker Leon Gaillard who lived at DuPont and Broadway in San Francisco in 1869-70, her 1874 and 1887 inventions dealing with Combined needle and cord for shoe-sewing may also be mechanical (or related); i.e., for a shoe-sewing machine.

Harriet Hosmer (1830-1908): Five patents (or applications), one American and four British: an Improved process of making artificial marble (U.S., 1879), and four for Obtaining motive power and Motive-power engines (Brit., 1878-81). Hosmer first pursued a career in sculpture, and was 48 when she got her first patent. Even as a child, however, she was noted for inventing "little machines and ingenious household devices."

Only (surviving) child of a wealthy family, she became financially independent when her father died in 1862, but continued to work professionally as a sculptor while also inventing. Her art was much more visible than her inventions until about 1880, when her sculpture output slowed as she became fascinated with magnetic motors and perpetual motion. For almost thirty years, till her death in 1908, she invented and experimented mainly in this area.[11]

Amanda Theodosia Jones (1835-1914): One of only three women mentioned as inventors by *Notable American Women* (*NAW*/1), was also known as poet, spiritualist, and entrepreneur. In 1872, with a male collaborator, she invented the vacuum canning process (and

---

[11]Information here comes from *NAW*/1, and from an undated interview with Hosmer in the New York *Evening Post*, sent me by the Schlesinger Library ("Miss Hosmer's Discoveries").

some of its apparatus), getting five patents in 1873, at age 38. At 45, she patented a Liquid fuel burner (1880). Over the next twenty years she invented Jones' Master Valves for oil burners (no patents found; possibly kept as trade secrets and sold to oil companies), as well as the Ready-Opener tin can (possibly trademarked rather than patented). In 1904 Jones at last patented a Valve. By now she was nearly 70. She received five more patents before her death—two in 1905, one in 1906, one in 1912, and one in 1914—for food-preparation apparatus and fuel burners, including a Liquid-fuel furnace. At that last patent, she would have been nearly 80. Thus, her inventive career, as gauged by patent dates, began when she was 38 and spanned more than 40 years.

Daughter of a master weaver and his widely read wife, reared in a family of modest means but culturally rich, Jones must be accounted middle class. She never married, supporting herself by occupations ranging from spiritual healing to writing to invention and business. Most pertinent here is the Woman's Canning and Preserving Company she founded in Chicago in 1890 to exploit her canning process. She is one of a very few women publicly acknowledged as inventors in the 19th Century, the only one so classified by the *DAB* (first series).

Margaret Knight (1838-1914): At least 24 patents, plus a great many unpatented inventions, including one she created at twelve. Counting that unpatented childhood invention—adopted throughout New England's textile industry—her inventive career spans more than sixty years. Knight's inventions are fairly diverse, but her patents are mostly for heavy machinery, clustered in three areas: paper-bag manufacturing, shoe-manufacturing, and rotary engines. Indeed, most of her patents dealt with manufacturing; her rotary engines evidently drove production machines rather than vehicles. She was still inventing full tilt in her 70s. In fact, she told a *New York Times* interviewer in 1913 that she was working 20 hours a day on her 89th invention. This at 75, only a year before her death (Janeway, 1978, pp. 55-6; see also *NAW*/1).

Knight probably came from a working-class family, as her brothers worked in a textile mill. She never married, supporting herself by working for manufacturing companies and by her inventions. Obituary notices called her a "woman Edison." The comparison is apt in professionalism, but not in lasting fame or financial reward, for she died with an estate of less than $300. She allegedly refused $50,000 for her paper-bag-folding machine (Smith, Apr. 1891: 4) — which also won her the Royal Legion of Honor from Queen Victoria (1871) — and doubtless sold other inventions, but must have spent the money from one invention on developing the next (Janeway, 1978: 55-6).

Bertha A. Lammé (1869-1943): Lammé is the one documented employed professional inventor in the sample, and the important motors, generators, and other large machines she helped design during her twelve years at Westinghouse could number over 100. She was recognized by Westinghouse as a successful design engineer (n.d.) and by the public as "the particular star among American women electricians [professionals in electrical engineering]," in an article appearing in both the *New York Sun* and the *Woman's Journal* (Nov. 26, 1899; Dec. 1899); and the business of the team on which she worked was to invent new machines. Yet she held no patents.

Bertha Lammé, from a prosperous Ohio farm family, had an older brother for a mentor, and became the first woman to graduate from Ohio State University in engineering. On marrying, she left engineering (Holzer, 1983).

Mary Jane Montgomery: Montgomery's known patents were few, and granted in a short span of time (1864-6). However, they are of a type — an Improved war vessel, an Improvement in locomotive wheels, and an Improved apparatus for punching corrugated metals — that could scarcely be whipped up in one's kitchen, and as late as 1903 a *Scientific American* writer called her the "one professional woman inventor in America" ("Women Inventors," Apr. 4, p. 247). This suggests that she continued inventing, if not patenting, after the 1860s. Both the Shaker *Manifesto* in 1890 (July, p. 164), and the *Scientific American* writer mention "other devices" she invented or "a number of other patents" that she held, and both note that she made money from her inventions.

Mary S. (c.1851-80): Like Bertha Lammé, Mary S. held no patents in her own name. However, Charlotte Smith, who knew her in St. Louis in the 1870s, says Mary created 53 inventions in her short life, profitably patented by the attorneys and patent agents who bought them from her for $5-10 (April 1891, p. 2). Since these knowledgeable men bought her inventions, they must have been commercially viable, probably mostly mechanical. Mary S.'s father was an inventor, and she learned from him; indeed some of her inventions were completions of things he began.

Emily E. Tassey (1823-99): Five patents, 1876-80: an Improved apparatus for raising sunken vessels, two Improvements in siphon propeller-pumps, one for Propulsion of vessels, and a Dredging machine. As I point out elsewhere,[12] the last two patents, both granted in 1876, were omitted by LWP. Tassey was 53 at her first patent.

Tassey was descended from the prominent Evans family of McKeesport, Pennsylvania. Since she married a lawyer and herself taught secondary school (sometimes running a school of her own), I consider her middle class. Her husband died young, and she needed to support herself and her three children. All of her patents were granted after widowhood.[13]

Harriet R. Tracy: Harriet Tracy had at least 16 patents in her own name and, as noted above, possibly one more in another woman's name.[14] Most of her patents dealt with sewing machines, e.g., a Loop-taker, a Feeding mechanism, and two Shuttle-actuating mechanisms. However, she also patented a Crib attachment for bedsteads (1868), a Fire escape, and two elevator inventions. Tracy's gravity elevator was installed in the Woman's Building at the Chicago World's Fair of 1892-3 (Weimann, 431).

Since her patents span 25 years and few women likely received patents before age 25, she was probably at least 50 at her last patent.

Further dividing these professional inventors into employed and

---

[12]In a paper presented at a conference on women, work and technology at the University of Connecticut at Storrs (Stanley, 1984). A revised version is Stanley, 1987.

[13]Biographical information on Tassey was furnished by Eunice J. Emery of the Carnegie Free Library of McKeesport (1987).

[14]That other woman was Ellen Curtis Demorest, herself an inventor-co-inventor, in fact, of tissue-paper patterns for dressmaking, among other things—but mainly known as an entrepreneur and fashion arbiter of late-19th-century America. For an attempt to unravel this puzzling situation, see my forthcoming book *Mothers of Invention*.

independent samples is not valid here, as only **Bertha Lammé** belongs unequivocally in the employed category. I suspect that **Mildred Blakey** worked for pipe- and tube-manufacturers, either in house or as a consultant, but have as yet no proof. **Margaret Knight** also worked for two or three companies, but evidently went independent as soon as possible, and remained independent for the rest of her life.

Age of professional inventors. Where I know birth dates, I can calculate with some certainty the age range of inventive creativity, as marked by patents. For the others, I estimate by assuming an age of 25 at first patent—which seems conservative, given the cost of a patent. Excluding the two (Lammé and Mary S.) who held no patents in their own names, the ages for the professional sample are shown in Table 2.

As can be seen, where the age at first patent is known, it is much higher than 25. In fact, using only those six inventors of known age, *the average age at first patent is nearly 40 (39.2), and the average age at last patent nearly 65 (64.5).* Thus 25 may be too conservative a figure for estimated age at first patent. Using 39 (as for known ages) instead of 25, for example, we get an estimated average age at last patent of 61. The combined average of known and estimated ages at last patent, even using 25 for the estimate, is nearly 56 (55.75).

These prolific inventors[15] are a highly interesting sample. Until recently, professional women inventors were held not to exist, certainly not in the 19th Century. Let us now compare them with a second group, part of a larger group of women inventors exhibiting their inventions at the Philadelphia Centennial of 1876, analyzed about ten years ago by Deborah Warner. Warner does not call any of these women professional inventors,[16] though she says that most of the women were at the Centennial to make money.

---

[15]"Prolific," of course is a relative term. Marjorie Ciarlante considers an inventor prolific at 20 inventions in one of her groups. My "prolific" threshold for 19th-century women inventors is five patents/inventions. Montgomery is included because it seems clear that she has more inventions to her credit than her three patents would indicate.

[16]Mary Carpenter, one of the Professional Inventors sample just discussed, exhibited at the Centennial, but is not included in the comparison sample.

TABLE 2

AGE AT FIRST AND LAST PATENTS FOR
12 PROFESSIONAL WOMEN INVENTORS, 19TH C. U.S.

	Age @ 1st pat.	Span of patents *	Age @ last patent**
Alexander	[25]	1857-82 - 26 yrs incl.	[50]
Beasley	31	1878-98 - 21 yrs "	51
Blakey	[25]	1874-1904 - 31 yrs "	[55]
Blanchard	33	1873-1915 - 43 yrs "	75
Carpenter	[25]	1862-94 - 33 yrs "	[57]
Gaillard	[25]	1874-92 - 19 yrs "	[43]
Hosmer	48	1878-81 - 4 yrs "	51
Jones	38	1873-1914 - 42 yrs incl.	79
Knight	32	1870-1912 - 43 yrs "	74
Montgomery	[25]	1864-6 - 3 yrs incl.	[27]
Tassey	53	1876-80 - 5 yrs "	57
Tracy	[25]	1868-93 - 26 yrs "	[50]

Av. age @ 1st patent:	known	39.2
	est.	25
Av. age @ last patent		
known		64.5
est. (25 @ 1st patent)		47
comb. known & estimated		55.75
(using 25 @ 1st patent)		
guided est. (39 @ last patent)		61

  *Inclusive figures used because patents were granted in both
first and last years; age at last patent will be one year less
than sum of age at first patent and years of patent span.
  **Bracketed figures are estimates.

CENTENNIAL SAMPLE (1876)

I will not describe these Centennial women in much detail, as
Warner has ably discussed them in Martha Trescott's pathbreaking
anthology *Dynamos and Virgins Revisited* (Warner, 1979). Further
information about some of them will appear in my forthcoming
book *Mothers of Invention* (Stanley, 1989). Creators of 79 inventions, they answered Mrs. Gillespie's call for inventions, filling
25% of the space in the Woman's Pavilion! Their inventions range
from minor convenience items to a night-signaling invention

adopted by most of the world's navies, and **Margaret Colvin**'s Triumph rotary washing machine. Warner considers the women a cross-section of the American middle class, which she says was experiencing considerable economic instability just then.

Most interesting, however, as with the Professional Inventors sample, is the age at which these women received their patents. Since most of these women had only one patent, we cannot look at a patent span, but only at age on receiving the Centennial patents. Thus the only inventors who can be used in the tabulation are those 15 women whose birthdates are known (or can be reasonably estimated).

As can be seen from this sample (Table 3), women's age at first patent (or first independent patent or Centennial patent)[17] is high. At 42 it is higher than that (39.2) of the Professional Inventors sample just discussed. If we throw out the one most unusual age of 28, the average age of these Centennial inventor-exhibitors at first or Centennial patent is nearly 44 (43.7).

What explains this interesting phenomenon?

DISCUSSION AND ANALYSIS

Two questions immediately arise:

1. What should be the average age at first patent for a roughly comparable group of *male* inventors?
2. What accounts for the difference in age at first patent between the two women's samples?

---

[17]Things are somewhat more complex than can be represented here. **Ellen Demorest**, for example, had several inventions to her credit, but virtually none of them were patented, at least in her own name. Warner mentions four patents for **Margaret Colvin**, but Colvin may have invented numerous improvements for her washers, which were evidently manufactured for some years; she may even have had other patents, as I have accepted Warner's figure here and not done a complete search. **Dr. Elizabeth French** held only one patent, which presumably covered a whole complex of electrotherapeutic equipment. As electrotherapy was her specialty, she may have invented many improvements in her apparatus without bothering to get further patents.

TABLE 3

CENTENNIAL SAMPLE
AGE AT RECEIPT OF CENTENNIAL PATENTS
FOR 15 WOMEN INVENTOR-EXHIBITORS

Name	Birthdate+	Patent date	Age
Sarah Ball	1844	1876	32
Mary Jackson	1837	1876	39
Sarah Bancroft	1824	1874	50
Mary Blauvelt	1832	1873	41
Caroline Brooks	1840	1877	37
Laura Chapman	1838	1874	36
Margaret P. Colvin	1828	1871	43
Martha Coston	1820-1*	1871++	51#
Ellen Demorest	1825	1882	57
Mary Evard	1825	1868	43
Elizabeth French	1821*	1875	54
Ann Graham	1832	1870	38
Ellen Griswold	1821	1867	46
Charlotte Sterling	[1827]	1872	45
Emma Whitman	1845	1873	28
		Average age	42

+As given by Warner (1979).

*The bracketed date is an estimate. An asterisk marks an age learned from other sources. Coston's date is from her autobiography (1886). I assume Sterling was about the same age as her husband, who Warner says was born in 1827. French's age is from her obituary and from census records (Gribble, 1983).

++This was Coston's first independent invention (an earlier patent realized an idea of her husband's), and the patent that brought her to the Centennial.

#Coston gives no firm birth date, but tells how old she was at certain events; thus a slight uncertainty here.

Regarding (1) let us look at the 170 "eminent" American inventors studied by Marjorie Ciarlante (1978, Table 3-1). Although Ciarlante focuses on antebellum inventive activity, the men's active dates probably overlap enough with the women's to provide a pertinent comparison. The men received their first patents on the average *seven years younger* (at 32) than did the Professional Inventors sample (39.2) among the women, and *10 years younger* than did the Centennial sample (42).

Even more interesting, the 16 Single-item inventors among the men (arguably most comparable with the Centennial sample) showed the highest average age at first patent (36.25) of the four groups of men, with the 43 Eclectic inventors averaging only 28.7 years, and the 81 Specialized and 30 Semi-eclectic inventors coming in between with 33.4 and 31.8 years, respectively (Ciarlante defines these groups on pp. 35-6). Invention, in short, may begin well before 40 for 19th-century men.

As for the second question, let us note at once that the difference in age at first patent between the two women's samples is small. Since the samples are also small, their significance is unclear. The main point, in any case, is that for both groups of women, invention begins relatively late in life, and that in this regard two otherwise rather different groups of women are more similar to each other than to a group of male inventors.[18]

A more striking difference between the two women's samples is in *number of patents* held. In contrast to the Centennial women's single patents, the Professional sample had from 3 to 53 patents each, for an average of more than 15. If we throw out both Mary S. and Bertha Lammé (whose many contributions were patented by others) the average is still slightly over 11.[19]

Another striking difference between the Professional and Centennial samples that both deserves pointing out for its own sake, and

---

[18]Lest we dismiss it too lightly, however, it should be noted that the life expectancy for women as late as 1900 was only 48 years (California Commission on the Status of Women, 1985, no. 3, p. 1).

[19]Comparable figures for males from Ciarlante's samples (1979, pp. 78-9) for 170 male inventors mentioned in *DAB* were 4.77 for Specialized, 5.81 for Semi-eclectic, and 5.28 for Eclectic Inventors, for an overall average of 5.16. Among *DAB* inventors with four or more patents, somewhat more comparable to the Professional women's sample, the respective figures were 9.94, 6.45, 8.41, and an overall average of 8.20. Among *DAB* inventors with nine or more patents, the respective figures were 14.44, 13.00, 13.29, with an average of 13.75 patents per inventor.

may help explain the other two observed differences, is marital status.

Deborah Warner says that about 25% of the overall Centennial sample were widows or spinsters (1979, p. 105).[20] Thus, some 75% were married.[21] Roughly the same proportion prevails in the select Centennial sample of 15 women examined here: one is single, two are definitely and one probably widowed, and the rest are married.

Among my professional inventors, on the other hand, the proportion of widows and spinsters is *at least* 50%: five were life-long spinsters, a sixth (**Lammé**) was single during her entire professional career, and a seventh (**Tassey**) was definitely a widow at the time of all her patents. If we count **Montgomery**, who was probably a spinster,[22] **Beasley**, who may have been a widow during her patent span (the Philadelphia directory [1877-1904] and census records [1880, 1900] are contradictory), and **Carpenter**, who I conclude was single for some two-thirds of her patent span,[23] the probable total for widows and spinsters in the professional sample rises to 10 out of 14, or 71% — virtually the reverse of the percentage for the Centennial sample.

---

[20]Warner bases her percentages on 79 women, whereas there were actually 82 (79 inventions, but three had two patentees), but 25% is not far off. If Mary Nolan, who is left undesignated in Warner's text and appendix, but who was actually single, is added to those designated "Miss," and the resulting total of 13 single women is added to the 7 widows or probable widows, the total of widows and spinsters equals 20, or 24.4% of the Centennial exhibitors.

[21]Aside from the widows, Warner designates only 46 of the women as Mrs. (56.1%); the remaining 17 are undesignated (the two given the title of Madame are corset-makers who used the title professionally; they may or may not have been married). However, Warner has evidently counted them as married in order to arrive at approximately 75%.

[22]Both Ida Tarbell (1887, p. 356) and the *Scientific American* (1903, 247) call her "Miss Montgomery."

[23]Warner calls her "Mrs. Carpenter," but the *Scientific American* calls her "Miss Carpenter" (1870, p. 164); and there is a Miss M. P. Carpenter — a teacher — in the San Francisco city directories at the right time (1869) for her San Francisco patents. Warner mentions a marriage, after which she became Mrs. Mary P. C. Hooper. By then, Carpenter had already received eight of her 13 patents. This could have been a re-marriage; but note the nine-year hiatus between her last patent as Carpenter (1876) and her first as Hooper (1885).

CONCLUSION

Considerable further research remains to be done, to learn the birthdates of more of these inventors; to establish and unravel the effects of class or economic background, marriage, childbearing, and other life-stage influences. However, even though these samples are small, I suspect that they may turn out to be fairly representative, and we can truly say that, for women, invention begins at 40. Moreover, if these two groups are representative, we can suggest that invention begins later for women than for men, and, among women, later for the occasional than for the professional woman inventor. There are hints that the inventive profession, like others in the received wisdom of the 19th Century, might not have mixed well with marriage.

Most exciting of all, inventive creativity can continue late in life. In the Professional Inventors sample, it continued 13 years past the life expectancy for women at the end of the 19th Century. If the same relationship pertains today, women who survive that long may expect to invent into their 90s.

REFERENCES

[Where not otherwise specified, information and data used in this paper come from United States or British patent records, or my forthcoming book on women inventors.]

[Blanchard, H.A.] (1922, January 13). Obituary. Portland (ME) *Evening Express and Advertiser*, p. 39.
Carpenter self-threading and self-setting needle for sewing machines (1870, September 10). *Scientific American*, 164.
Ciarlante, M.H. (1979). *A statistical profile of eminent American inventors, 1700-1860*. Unpublished Ph.D. dissertation, Northwestern University [1978].
Coston, M.C. (1886). *A signal success: The work and travels of Mrs. Martha J. Coston*. Philadelphia, PA: Lippincott.
Gribble, K.J. *Searching for women who lost their names*. Paper presented at the National Women's Studies Association Conference, Columbus, OH.
Holzer, G. (1983). *Bertha Lammé; First woman electrical engineer*. Unpublished paper sent to me by the author.
James, E.T., James, J.W., and Boyer, P.S. (1971). *Notable American women*

1607-1950: A biographical dictionary. Cambridge, MA: Harvard University Press.

LWP: See United States Patent Office.

Shaker *Manifesto* (1890, July). Untitled article, *20*, 7, 164.

Smith, C. (1891, April). *The Woman Inventor*, No. 1.

———. (1891, June). *The Woman Inventor*, No. 2.

Stanley, A. (1989). *Mothers of invention: Notes for a revised history of technology*. Metuchen, NJ: Scarecrow, 1989.

———. (1984). *A rose by any other name: Omissions and dysclassifications in a list of 19th-century American women patentees, 1876 and 1890*. A paper presented at the Conference on Women, Work & Technology, University of Connecticut, Storrs, CT.

———. (1987). The patent office clerk as conjuror: The vanishing-lady trick in a 19th-century historical source. In Barbara Wright (Ed.), *Transformations: Women, work & technology*. Ann Arbor: University of Michigan Press.

Tarbell, I. (1887). Women as inventors. *The Chautauquan*, 7, 6, 355-7.

Trescott, M.M. (In preparation). *New images, new paths: Women engineers in American history in their own words*.

United States Patent and Trademark Office (1888). *Women inventors to whom patents have been granted by the United States government, 1790 to July 1, 1888*. Washington, DC: Government Printing Office; with updates to March 1, 1895.

Warner, D.J. (1979). Women inventors at the centennial. In Martha Trescott (Ed.), *Dynamos and virgins revisited*. Metuchen, NJ: Scarecrow Press.

Westinghouse Electric Co., Public Relations Dept. (n.d.). Benjamin C. Lammé. Unpublished manuscript sent to me by Guenter Holzer.

Weimann, J.M. (1981). *The fair women: The story of the woman's building, world's Columbian exposition*. Chicago, IL: Academy Chicago.

Willard, F.E., and Livermore, M.A. (1893). *A woman of the century: 1470 biographical sketches . . . of leading American women. . . .* Buffalo, NY: Moulton.

Women in electricity. (1899, November 26). *New York Sun*.

Women inventors. (1903, April 4). *Scientific American*. p. 247.

Inventing Freedom:
The Positive Poetic "Mutterings"
of Older Women

Jo C. Searles

SUMMARY. Poetry by older women is now appearing with increasing frequency in journals, magazines, and newsletters. It reaches a wide audience and defines areas of experience formerly ignored: the pains and pleasures of women as they grow older and their various attitudes and solutions to the aging process. The news is positive; their poems are affirmative, strong, and inspiring.

And I will speak . . .
more and more in crazy gibberish . . .
witches' incantations, poetry, old women's mutterings,
schizophrenic code, accents, keening . . .
and whatever else will invent
this freedom.

—Robin Morgan
"Monster" (1961)

In the year it was published, Robin Morgan's poem was a revolutionary cry. It still is. Who needs "witches' incantations" and "old women's mutterings"? Certainly they have been absent from the consciousness of American culture. Few, if any, women over forty are pictured on TV commercials. Little space is given in traditional

Jo C. Searles, Assistant Professor of English and Women's Studies at Penn State Altoona, specializes in women's literature and spirituality. She has worked with Carol Christ, Starhawk, and Jean Houston in the USA and has done research in Brazil, Greece, and Malaysia.

sociological and psychological texts to that age group—check a few tables of contents for yourself. As for the traditional canon of literature taught in colleges and universities, the works of women now entering the mainstream describe the Black experience, the chicana, occasionally the Native-American, but even in Women's Studies, there are few materials that focus on the special worlds of older women.

We have been slow to speak, slow to insist on being heard. There are reasons. Witches' words lack respectability; old women's opinions are discounted. Ntozake Shange's description of a Black woman's muteness (1977), "she's been dead so long/ closed in silence so long/ she doesn't know the sound/ of her own voice" (p. 3) could well stand for a diffidence that has muffled our own utterances. Not only does society impose silence on us; we impose it on ourselves. In "It Must," Ruth Fainlight (1980) demonstrates that process:

> Friends, sisters, are you used to your face in the mirror?
> Can you accept or even recognize it?

> *   *   *   *   *

> Now, I long to ask my friends these very
> questions and compare reactions, blurt out
> the taboo words. But we're so polite, so lavish
> with compliments, tender, protective—cherishing
> the common hurt. . . . (pp. 76-77)

The words, taboo as they still are, reflect the difficulty that women have in recognizing and coming to terms with their own aging.

Much of that difficulty, that "common hurt," is self-imposed, but it reflects the assumptions of our society that equate personality with the rosy blush of youth; unlike the furrows and experience-lines that suggest male wisdom, wrinkles on female faces signify a descent into passivity and senility. Note, for instance, the uneasy attitude of young Val in Gina Berriault's (1982) short story, "Nocturne." She is uncomfortable with the presence of Eulalia, an old woman who comes by Val's mother-in-law's apartment to beg genteelly for food:

Ah, God, will I look like that? An old woman, she thought, is more piteous than an old man because she is less pitied, for there is something like a betrayal about a woman's growing old, she seems to be betraying her own nature. (p. 227)

Val's uneasiness stems from a deeper cause than pity for Eulalia: well aware of her own mortality, it is her own aging that Val mourns for. The societal depersonalization that she fears, however, is feeling the healthy stresses of change.

As the years of vital life lengthen and we begin to feel lusty, active, and worthwhile, we are defining our lives in new terms. Maggie Kuhn, who founded the Gray Panthers at age 65, rejects the term "senior citizen" because she considers it "a euphemism . . . , part of the denial." She adds, "I just call myself an old woman, and I say it with trumpets. I have survived!" (p. 6). That spirit informs and inspires a host of declarations that are beginning to surface in both popular and literary media, declarations that will eventually make accessible to all ages the pains, pleasures, and values of older and *old* women, who form an ever-larger part of the world's population.

That Robin Morgan included *poetry* in her list of "whatever . . . will invent/ this freedom" is not surprising, for poetry, well-done and widely-distributed, can be revolutionary. Its appeal is immediate; it sticks in the spiritual craw and produces the continuing irritation that leads to real change. It also creates the images by which the self can be defined and can face the world—face and transform it. That poetry is now being written. Alicia Ostriker (1986) speaks triumphantly of the "extraordinary tide of poetry by American women in our own time . . . explicitly female in the sense that writers have chosen to explore experiences central to their sex and to find forms and styles appropriate to their exploration" (p. 7).

Poems of age form a strong undercurrent of that "extraordinary tide." Already they are found in both academic journals and popular magazines and newsletters; their forms and styles ranging from erudite and complex poetry to simple verse, their attitudes a melange of pessimism, optimism, bitchiness, and celebration. No surprise, this—age brings no more unanimity to its possessors than any other phenomenon of life.

The earliest and most obvious effect of passing years, physical change, triggers Nikki Giovanni to remark, "i know my upper arms will grow/ flabby it's true/ of all the women in my family" and Sibyl James (1986) to add, "The nose will spread./ The elbows flap and fold like rhino's knees" (p. 89). Yet, perhaps strangely in a culture still youth-oriented, women writers don't seem to mind those cosmetic disasters. Erica Jong (1968), whose "Aging (balm for a 27th birthday)" deplores the process — "ruin proceeds downward/ lingering for a while around the mouth hardening the smile/ into prearranged patterns (irreversible!) writing furrows/ from the wings of the nose" — concludes with a suggestion that rather than trying to censor those changes, it might be better to lie back and listen, "letting the years make love the only way (poor blunderers)/ they know" (pp. 45-46).

Going further, some women find their altered appearance not only acceptable, but exciting. Nancy Corson Carter (1986), for instance, sees it as an "Unmasking": "At 40 I can drop the masks. . . ."

> Why romanticize the Goddess?
> After I've lived Maiden and Mother
> I get to try Hag —
>
> Her beauty goes deeper than diets or cold creams;
> She's the fierce fiery free one asleep in my core;
> I'm old enough now to let her BE, wide awake! (n.p.)

These are declarations, often in the first person, with their own insistent beauty, a sense of pride in the battle scars so hardly won. Many have a straightforward stance, directly addressing the world, that makes them accessible to a wide audience and well-adapted for public reading. Picture an audience well-groomed and dressed for an evening in public confronted with the celebration of physical "deformity" trumpeted in Irma McClaurin's "These Graying Women":

> These graying women with braided hair
> whose tobacco lips are snarled tightly,
> whose rounded shoulders and bunioned feet
> have walked long years;

*   *   *   *   *

these women shall be our salvation. (p. 26)

Images like these, pictures that force us to awareness of different visions of physical change, provide an understanding that Berriault's Val was lacking. We are not, as she felt, "betraying [our] own nature"; we are *creating* it. As Elsen Lubetsky insists in her conclusion to "Statement,"

> It's time we gave witness,
> attention, attention must be paid,
> or we'll march hand in hand,
> together strong as a battering ram,
> create situations until others
> understand we're not designed
> to rust. Some day they'll be us. (n.p.)

The situations created in this new kaleidoscope of women's older years are a melange of experiences: being with others, seeking solitude; meeting new challenges, settling happily into beloved spaces; caring for relatives, being dependent on them; finding meaning in familiar rituals, rejecting tradition in favor of maverick independence. Yet all seem informed by a hard-won realism, the attitude voiced by Susan A. Katz (1987) in "New Directions," that "weary of explanations,/ at mid-life I am more comfortable/ with the truth" (p. 71).

In her time, Emily Dickinson's published poems were cleaned up for public consumption, their edges polished and made presentable for readers not comfortable with her hard truths. A century later, women poets are brandishing the two-edged sword of age and rejoicing as it glints through the chilly air. Like her, they reject the stuffiness of the Cambridge ladies' drawing room, of the dowagers with snow-white, netted hair. Anne Cameron (1985) goes further when she characterizes Old Woman as one who "does not bake/ gingerbread or apple pie/ . . . and say Oh my you poor dear/ while patting your hand/ and promising/ a better life in heaven." Instead of providing tea and sympathy, she suggests unsettling mystery:

> With Old Woman
> you provide your own

tea or coffee
   — or whatever —
you either talk
or you don't
   she stares
   her eyes boring
   into your soul
she may hum or whistle
a tune you think you recognize

she promises
nothing. (p. 51)

Nothing — and everything. Cameron's definition brings an intriguing whiff of the unknowns that exist in our uncharted territories of later years.

Most exciting and promising is the surge of positive energy that fills this wave of poetry. We hug ourselves and each other. We admire our silver hair and work-hardened muscles. We value the knowledge and perspective that the years have given us. The decades cease to be threatening as we welcome their possibilities; even the big-0's are positive occasions. Speaking of 5-0, Roberta Harper Roberts (1982) comments, with an air of surprise, that "the cloak of the fifth decade" seems to fit. It is warm, comfortable, and can be worn anywhere. She concludes,

So unique a garment
     that it is unimportant that it has become wrinkled and
faded
     by smiles, and tears, and time.

Not only does it fit — it triggers an impromptu scene where she finds herself "All dressed up, laughing aloud/ WITH myself,/ enjoying the music" (n.p.).

So we are beginning to go beyond acceptance of the years, beyond welcome even, to a yeasty celebration — of ourselves, our powers, our earth. The emerging portrait of women is neither traditional nor tame; in fact, it is frequently sensuous and rowdy. We can relax and absorb through thinning skins the daily miracles of our world. Marge Piercy (1988) declares, "At fifty, the sun, the

moon, the tides,/ the seasons rule me like a field gone wild"
(p. 60). And Lucille Clifton (1980), whose jaunty acceptance of her
solid body and Kali-spirit shines through her poems, describes the
"green girl/ in a used poet" who will "break through gray hairs/
into blossom"

> and her lovers will harvest
> honey and thyme
> and the woods will be wild
> with the damn wonder of it. (p. 8)

This world of poetry is, it seems to me, something new under the
moon. Through its variety of forms and multiplicity of viewpoints,
it promises not only the delineation of experience formerly unknown, but a new definition of elderly female wisdom formed of
the wise/wild blood of its writers. Marge Piercy's advice (1988) in
"Loving the Crone" that "If we do not honor wisdom, we are
doomed/ to stupidity" (p. 29) suggests Ruth Harriet Jacob's description (1982) of a friend: "At seventy/ you grasp wisdom/ in
your hands/ while they are still strong."

Gradually, gradually, as these poems, many others, and those yet
to be written become part of our heritage, we will invent the freedom envisioned by Robin Morgan and join in Sarah Lairo's praise
(1987) of age:

> Old Woman, You give me the courage to live my life in
> freedom. Though the vision of You is sometimes frightening,
> the laughter in your eyes dares me to live boldly.

> *   *   *   *   *

> You are the silence in the Way I walk. Wisdom comes when
> I am calm enough to listen. In those moments when I am Your
> echo, I understand. (p. 12)

REFERENCES

Berriault, G. (1982). *The infinite passion of expectation*. San Francisco: North
Point Press.

Cameron, A. (1985). Old woman. *Earth witch*. (p. 51) Madeira Park, B.C.,
Canada: Harbour Publishing.

Carter, N. C. (1985, September-October). Unmasking. *Broomstick*, n.p.

Clifton, L. (1980). What the mirror said. *Two-headed woman*. (p. 8) Amherst: University of Massachusetts Press.

Fainlight, R. (1980). *Sibyls and others*. London, England: Hutchinson & Co.

Jacobs, R. H. (1982, September-October). For Joan's 70th birthday. *New Directions for Women*, n.p.

James, S. (1986). Poem for Samantha and me. In J. Alexander, D. Berrow, L. Domitrovich, M. Donnelly, and C. McLean (Eds.). *Women and aging* (p. 89). Corvallis, OR: Calyx Books.

Jong, E. (1968). *Fruits & vegetables*. New York: Holt, Rinehart and Winston.

Katz, S. (1987). New directions. *When I am an old woman I shall wear purple*. (p. 71) Manhattan Beach, CA: Papier-Mache Press.

Kuhn, M. (1989). Celebrating life: an interview with Maggie Kuhn. *Peace and freedom*, *49*(1), 6-7.

Lairo, S. (1987). Hag's song. *Stardust Salamander*, *2*(1), 12.

Lubetsky, E. (n.d.) Statement. *Broomstick*, n.p.

McClaurin, I. (n.d.) These graying women. *Voices of women: Poetry by and about third world women*. (p. 26) New York: Women's International Resource Exchange.

Ostriker, A. (1986). *Stealing the language: The emergence of women's poetry in America*. Boston: Beacon Press.

Piercy, M. (1988). *Available light*. New York: Alfred A. Knopf.

Roberts, R. H. (1982, November/December) Happy birthday to those of us . . . *Broomstick*, n.p.

Shange, N. (1977). *For colored girls who have considered suicide when the rainbow is enuf*. New York: Macmillan.

Index

Adolescence
  of midlife lesbians, 112-116
  and creativity, 134
Adult children
  and aged parents, 7
  as companions for parents, 23,32
  and parental illness, 73,75,96,
    101-102
Advertising
  image of ideal woman and man,
    40
  gray-haired models in, 43
  TV commercials, 153
Alexander, Eliza, 136
Anger
  at loss of husband, 14,24
  of caregivers, 100,102-106
Appearance
  gray hair, 3,35-46
  "motherly", 37,38
  mixed messages about, 41-42,45
  of sexuality, 51
  and chemotherapy, 103
  and personality, 154
  upper arms, nose, elbows, 156
Arthur, Bea, 41

Baldwin, James, 39
Banner, Lois, 41
Beasley, Maria, 137,138,149
Berriault, Gina, 154
Blakey, Mildred, 137,138,144
Blanchard, Helen, 136,139
Boston Women's Health Collective,
  41

Cameron, Anne, 157,158
Caregiving
  in traditional marriage, 4,94ff
  emotional aspects, 37
  response to husband's illness, 73
  views of surviving spouses,
    93-107
Carpenter, Mary, 136,139
Carter, Nancy Corson, 156
Chodorow, Nancy, 82
Church
  and making friends, 10,31
  as volunteer activity, 13
Ciarlante, Marjorie, 147
Clifton, Lucille, 159
Colvin, Margaret, 146
Contratto, Susan, 82
Copper, Baba, 40
Creativity
  and family life, 5
  and writing, 10
  in poetry writing class, 24
  among midlife lesbians, 112,116
  and age, 134

Death
  and afterlife, 9,11
  and finances, 12
  and grief, 14
  of friends, 17,22
  male fears of, 38
  planning for, 85
  of spouse, 97,105
Divorce, 20
Dual-career family, 2,5,119-129